Holiness in an
Unholy Society

Holiness in an Unholy Society

Godly Living in Perilous Times

James A. Hambrick, Ph.D

WestBow
PRESS
A DIVISION OF THOMAS NELSON

WestBow Press books may be ordered through booksellers or by contacting:

WestBow Press
A Division of Thomas Nelson
1663 Liberty Drive
Bloomington, IN 47403
www.westbowpress.com
1-(866) 928-1240

Because of the dynamic nature of the Internet, any web addresses or links contained in this book may have changed since publication and may no longer be valid. The views expressed in this work are solely those of the author and do not necessarily reflect the views of the publisher, and the publisher hereby disclaims any responsibility for them.

Any people depicted in stock imagery provided by Thinkstock are models, and such images are being used for illustrative purposes only.

Certain stock imagery © Thinkstock.

ISBN: 978-1-4497-4568-4 (sc)
ISBN: 978-1-4497-4569-1 (hc)
ISBN: 978-1-4497-4567-7 (e)
Library of Congress Control Number: 2012906023

Printed in the United States of America

WestBow Press rev. date: 4/11/2012

In loving memory of my mother Joyce Ann Hambrick

Contents

"Where there is no counsel, the people fall; But in a multitude of counselors there is safety."

Proverbs 11:14

Preface

In twenty-five years of ministry and seventeen years in the law enforcement profession, I have witnessed many things. I have been privileged to have some wonderful experiences during this time, but I have also seen a decline in moral character and fortitude. Because of the same concern of others in our community, I was asked if I could come and speak to various groups of adults, teens, and youth of the challenges that we face in these times; after seeking direction from the Lord, I began to do a series entitled "Keeping it real, Holiness in an unholy society". This work is birth from the seminar and from the heart.

I want to thank the Holy Spirit for His leading in this project, and for all of those who gave inspiration and encouragement along the journey. There is nothing in this world that can make an impact on our hearts like the Word of God, as you meditate on these pages; I pray that you will hear His voice. May God bless you richly!

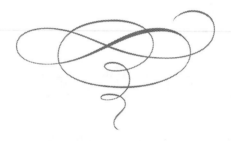

Acknowledgments

First and foremost, I want to thank my Lord and Savior Jesus Christ, for calling me out of darkness and into His marvelous light, for His deliverance, His Grace and Mercy that has been extended to me a wretch undone, I love you Lord! To my beautiful and loving wife Denise, for all of the love given and the support shown through the times when she might have felt neglected especially during the times of my scholastic studies, her understanding was tremendous and for that I am forever grateful. To our children: Thomasa, Antwain(Temeka), Donte(Jessie), Keyana, and Lashuana and our grandchildren: Sonia, Kalah, Sidney, Teyana, Endia, Tekia, Neveah, Erin, Christiana, Ariana1 and Ariana2.

I would also like to thank my brothers and sisters along with my entire family for all of the love and support that you've shown through the years, with a special thanks to my mother-in-law Lila, much love Mama! Also much thanks to all of you that have had a hand in the shaping of my life through rearing me. Pops (Greens and Fairways) Lillie, Aunt Mary, Uncle Fred (Aunt Dot), Aunt Pat (Uncle Bob), Uncle Ronny (Aunt Brenda), and to my Grandparents; Sarah Summers and James Summers (Deceased), Carroll Curtis Thomas (Deceased). To Mama Mattie and Ronnie Cartwright, I love you all. To all of my friends and co-laborers in ministry that I have gleaned from through the years, thank you for your friendship. To my co-workers, friends, and the many churches that I have had the privilege of worshiping together with, I will always cherish the moments.

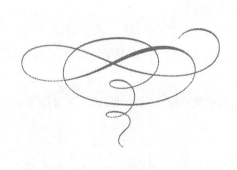

"In those days there was no king in Israel;

everyone did what right in his own eyes"

(Judges 21:25)

Introduction

Amongst the chaos, corruption and downward spiral, is there a place for holy living in our society? Where have we come from? Where do we want be? These are questions that need to be answered as we look into essence of this topic. There is a common understanding that things have changed in our society, and some it, not necessarily for the better. While we live in an age of vast technological advancement, better communication and media outlets, better equipment in various areas; including, but not limited to, military, schools, sports, industry, and science, there is a deep decline in the moral values by which we lived in times past.

There seems to be no regard for righteousness, and more concern for doing whatever seems right in one own eyes. But as it has been said, "just because everyone else is doing something, it doesn't make it right." Just take a look at current news events and you will be able to see this being played out right in front of your eyes by way of the activities in our nation's capitol, by the episodes that we constantly see from athletes, both college and professional, wall street and the mayhem there, our schools, and unfortunately our churches.

With so many advances that could help us in this country, we seem to be complacent with the downward spiral of our society. There is a lot of finger pointing, and enough blaming of others to go around, every day brings seemingly more questions than answers. The mentality is becoming more and more "do as I say, and not as I do," accountability is being thrown by the wayside, and mankind has become comfortable in doing his own thing, his own way and in his own time. Entitlement is the anthem of our day, as can be witnessed by the various scandals and controversies of today's time. We can sit back and be content with this type of living or we can take a stand and pursue righteousness and holiness. This popular culture doesn't have to be the accepted practice of all. I know that this book is not for everyone, it is for those who are tired of the way things are going and it's a word of encouragement to say that we don't have to be trapped by the woes and ills of those whose destiny is destruction. My prayer and desire is that we will rise up and take our place in the kingdom of God, which is not only in the bye and bye, but the here and now. I want you to be inspired by the word of God and be called to action to live holy lives in an unholy society.

"Therefore if the Son makes you free, you shall be free indeed" (John 8:36)

CHAPTER ONE

Freedom From Bondage

What happens when a young man who grew up in the church, from a background where going to church wasn't really an option, and was an all day event? From Sunday school to morning worship, then an afternoon service, maybe a little break until BTU (Bible Training Union), and Sunday night service. There was Wednesday bible study, Saturday choir rehearsal and a yearly dose of a week of VBS (Vacation Bible School). What happens when this young man takes to a life in the streets? Takes on the "ways of the world", becomes disengaged with what was once a very important piece of fabric that made up his being? Some might say that it was bound to happen because of burnout, others might offer that this is what you get when a child is forced to such living, and still there are others that +will add; that's what happens to PK's (Preacher's Kids).

You see, the young man I'm referring to is me, and during a part of my life we were raised by my uncle who was a preacher and a student at the seminary. We (siblings, cousins, and I) were taught in the scriptures and a godly life was modeled for us to follow and instructions for holy living and hard work were handed down. "Apply yourselves" was the word of the house, yet with all of this encouragement and instruction, I still found myself in a world of sin, making bad decisions and unwise choices in life. A child out of wedlock as a teenager, drugs, alcohol, etc; and all of this while still "going to Church".

This is just a small sample of my life and it would be tragic if these things only happened to me, but unfortunately it has happened to others, male and female alike; and now in the times we are living in it seems to be getting worse. Each generation has it vices and challenges that it faces, so there are those who discount it all by making statements like "that's just how it is". We cannot afford to feel comfortable with this kind of thinking, because the truth of the matter is that sin is still sin, but the stakes seemingly grow higher with each generation. Contrary to popular belief, "The wages of sin is still death", as recorded in the book of Romans chapter 6. Now that I have matured in the Lord and have a genuine relationship with Him, He has allowed me to see that there is a need for teaching and preaching in the area of holiness. Some say that this is a doctrine that is outdated and no longer relevant in our time, but that is so far from the truth. Unholy living is the decadence of our day and if we are not drawn back to holiness many will suffer needlessly and spend eternity in damnation.

Webster's definition of holiness is: (1) the state or quality of being holy; perfect moral integrity or purity; freedom from sin; sanctity; innocence. (2) The state of being hallowed, or consecrated to God or to His worship; sacredness. This will be expounded upon more as we go through this book, but one point that I want to make here is "quality", holiness is a quality, what type of qualities do we see from day to day? At work, at home, while we are out and about, and even while we are at church, what are we seeing? What are we hearing? And most of all what are we modeling? While we live in the wake of natural and manmade disasters such as 9/11, Katrina, Columbine, the Oklahoma City bombing, and many more unnamed at this time; there is another disaster that is much more prevalent in our time and it is called ungodliness. It is shown in our mannerism, our speech, our dress, and our attitude; it is being accepted more and more as the natural way of life. How will we ever get our young men to pull up their pants, or our young women to cover themselves and dress appropriately if we don't take a stand and set a standard that is based on holy living and holy principles?

This epidemic is not a race thing, it is not based upon any political affiliation, it's not based upon any social or economic standing, and it is certainly not based on any denominational preference. At its core, it affects us all because we all are a part of the society. It would be easy to say, "I'll just stay in my house and not let any of mess bother me" that would be fine if it were that simple, but what we are dealing with, I believe, is a spirit. A spirit that hinders growth in individuals, a spirit that robs people from enjoying the abundant living that Jesus said that He would give us, a spirit that enables and influences individuals to continue to walk in darkness, a spirit that is from the prince of darkness himself, and many are buying into his mindset that we can do no better. Like civilizations in times past we too have let other things become our gods; houses, automobiles, jewelry, jobs, drugs, money and even other people. We have become a society that wants to be constantly entertained so that we can somehow escape reality and not have to deal with the troubles that plague us, but after the entertainment we find ourselves back in the real world where destruction abounds. So what do we do? Where do we go? And to whom do we turn? All of these and more will be answered in the following pages, I hope you are ready for a ride, a ride that I pray will improve your life, give you instruction, encouragement, and provoke your heart so that you will answer the call to walk "HOLY IN A UNHOLY SOCIETY".

Let's Go!

We will never be able to walk in a life of holiness until we are free from bondage, and though the Emancipation of Proclamation was given long ago there are still many that are enslaved. Enslaved physically, mentally, and most important spiritually. Many people have become like zombies walking around just existing, with no real purpose, no hope, no aspirations or goals. There is no zeal in them to become anything other than what they are right now or to be in any other place than they are right now. They are in bondage and need to be freed, but there has to be a willingness to be free. Take a look at someone who is physically bond by drugs, until they come to the point where they really want to conquer the addiction, it will never happen. In those type of cases, one must be able to see themselves free. What we here most often is that they can't quit this or that and they are right to a certain extent, it takes the power of the Holy Spirit to break those yokes and chains. I know, because I was bound by various vices and was trying to quit in my on strength all the time but to no avail. It was not until I surrendered my life to the Lord and gave Him authority over my life that things began to change and the Holy Spirit began to do a work in me, on me, and through me, Praise God! And being that He is no respecter of persons, He can do the same in your life and the lives of others if you let Him. I have come to the knowledge and understanding that bondage or freedom is a choice. We must decide whether or not we want to be free, and if so, put ourselves in position to be free and that position is on our knees before and awesome God who loves us unconditionally. Remember that He, not us, has already paid in full the price for you and I to be free, the only thing that is required of us is to accept it. Drugs, alcohol, pornography and other sexual addictions, obesity, illiteracy, and many other vices plague our society and what makes this more alarming is it is beginning at a much earlier age than it used to. We are finding these things in our elementary schools ages now, but for many, because of being desensitized, there is no problem and all is well.

These are real issues with real consequences, and they will continue to hinder our progress if they are not addressed and dealt with properly. When I speak of an unholy society, just look at what our kids and grandkids are dealing with today, not only are drugs that are familiar to us by name such as marijuana, cocaine, and heroin prevalent, but also crack, crystal meth, ecstasy, and new synthetic drugs that are easily accessible to them. And to add to all of this, is the rampant misuse of prescription medication that these kids are getting right from home. Let's not be fooled into thinking that "my child wouldn't do anything like that". I am constantly finding myself in the presence of young teenagers and even preteens that have been to court and now required to do community service because of drug use and or possession. We have to wake up! We have to become more engaged in our children's lives and also become familiar with what's being presented to them when they are out of our presence. These kids are not just being targeted for the use of drugs, but also for the sell and distribution of them.

Can you compete with the glitz and glamour that is flaunted by individuals who make a living by being involved in the drug trade? The answer to that is no! Not on that level, what has to be conveyed to our children is what the bible has to say about a "good name" (***A good name is to be chosen rather than great riches, loving favor rather than silver and gold."(Proverbs 22:1*)**) We must warn of the consequences associated with the trappings of drugs, whether by use or selling. Furthermore, we must live by example and allow the Lord to work through us and be light to our children and to this dark world, it is not enough to just talk and tell others what not to do if they see us participating in the same things. We must be mindful of what the scripture says in relation to the accountability of children, (***Even a child is known by his doings, whether his work be pure, and whether it be right. Proverbs 20:11 NKJV***) So, there can be no excuse for them that choose to live lives of unrighteousness. God has given clear instructions in his word to live by, and if we are obedient, we can be successful in combating drugs in our lives and in the livves of others. There is a continuing shift especially with the youth of our society to experiment with all types of things for the sole purpose of getting high. I spoke of synthetic drugs, the new craze that is going on in America and abroad in Europe. Plant food, bath salts, incense, synthetic marijuana and other items are becoming more and more frequently used by them. It was stated by one of the youth in my community that they get twenty times higher with this new rage than with the traditional drugs, and the bad thing is that these are legal in most states and can be bought in stores and tobacco shops in communities nationwide. There have already been a number of reported overdoses and even deaths, from the use of these substances.

How long will we wait? How much death and pain has to occur before we do something to help save young hearts, minds, and souls. Go out and talk to these kids and you will get a sense that they feel nothing is wrong with what they are doing. It's almost as if they are saying, "we have a right to do what we want to do" and because of this attitude, there is very little respect for anyone in authority and parental guidance. Parents now are appreciated only for what they can provide by way of finances or material substance. Satan has brought this change in subtly and has seduced many minds but the scriptures state: *"There is a way that seems right to a man, but the end is the way of death."(Proverbs 14:12)* Those of us that have a relationship with the Father, through His Son Jesus Christ have to rise up and profess holiness, not just with lip service but with our lives. We must hold fast to the sacred teachings that we have from the creator of the universe who will never fail. His teachings are fail proof and always current, they are relevant to every generation and will stand forever. Believe them, trust them, and depend on them and most of all live by them! And as we do we remember that love is our motivation and the way by which we must spread the truth. People, especially the youth, desperately want someone to love them, even though it seem as though they don't. they are hurting and longing to be filled and satisfied, they just have not found what it is that has the capacity to do it. Just as catastrophic things are happening in our earth today; catastrophic things are happening in the lives of mankind. Many are the struggles of individuals today, and when you couple that with a failing economy, you get desperate people doing desperate things all in an attempt to survive. What is the answer to the madness?

We who are saved know the answer, and His name is Jesus. A life of holiness is what the Lord came to the earth to provide, by giving us an example by His own walk in the flesh as a man without sin. By His walk we are shown how to turn obstacles into opportunities and tragedies into triumph. There is the capacity within us to view our circumstances in a positive or negative light; unfortunately, most choose to do so negatively. They talk and complain about the situation instead of praying and focusing on what can be done to improve it. They are the ones that have a glass that is always half empty. The way of holiness is a positive way; it is a way that is measured by what the Lord can do and not what we can do in ourselves. Its knowing that with Him there is limitless possibilities. We must trust Him!

"Righteousness exalts a nation, But sin is a reproach to any people" (Proverbs 14:34)

CHAPTER TWO

A Nation in Crisis

B udget deficit, war conflict, stock market crash, health care and social security reform issues, high gas prices, and educational concerns just to name a few of the problems we face in this country at the present time. When will we wake up and realize that we cannot buy our way out of the crisis, we cannot spend our way out of it either. The democrats blame the republicans, the republicans point the finger at the democrats, The White House faults Congress, and Congress says the President is to blame. Where did we go so wrong? At what point did we get off of the right path?

This is what we know; our nation was founded on godly principal, it was established on sound doctrine and good moral values, but as time has gone by, we have seen rapid decay take place. Just think back for a minute if you are old enough to remember or have heard it talked about; a time where a man's word meant something, a hand shake was as good as any paper contract around in these times, neighbors looked out for one another, children looked up to and idolized their parents, sports heroes played for the love of the game, man what a forgotten concept. These were some of the values that we upheld and they were not compromised, then something changed that has profoundly affected the way we live, the way we treat one another, and the way we go about doing everyday routine things. Again, something changed and it has been interwoven into every fabric of our lives, it has carved a path of destruction along its route, it has brought a nation down to the appearance of mediocrity. Remember, I am talking about the greatest country on the face of the earth, the place where dreams could come true, the place of refuge where people from around the globe could come and make life good for themselves and their families. But now it seems the dream is turning to a nightmare, what happened? America is not without faults of its own, when we remember all of the positive things that were just mentioned, we are a nation that still has a degree of prejudices, people are still being judge based upon the color of their skin or ethnicity, but even before the advances that were made by African Americans and other groups there was still something about the values the we had and that were instilled in us as children. "Yes Sir, Yes Maam and No Sir, No Maam" have been replaced with "yeah and naw". Teachers didn't have to demand respect because they commanded respect. Now they are more or less regulated to a daytime babysitter. Parents today get beside themselves if the teacher tries to discipline their child even in a verbal way. My wife and I witnessed a horrific series of events as we visited my old high school one day. Students were talking back to and cursing the teachers, some were getting up and walking out of class, and some were even leaving the school grounds. This would not have been allowed in my day. We as a nation have fallen so low that there is a tolerance for just about anything. How do we think that we will prosper if this kind of attitude prevails? I am not saying that all kids are like this, but you go to the schools and witness for yourself, it is a growing percentage. Remember, we often say that this is our future; well, if there is not a change, the future looks bleak. Someone said, it all started when they took prayer out of schools, well that was an ill-advised thing to do but, you cannot take prayer out of the heart. You cannot take prayer of the mind and spirit, so as bad as it was and still is for prayer to be eliminated from various forums, prayer can never be eliminated from anyone unless they allow it. Just because there is a court order or new law passed that threatens holy living, don't think for one minute that we have to fold in the tent or throw in the towel because righteousness and holiness still and will always prevail. What happened? Scripture states *"Do not be deceived, God is not mocked; for whatever a man sows, that he will also reap." (Galatians 6:7)* Greed, envy, pride and self-righteousness come to mind when I think of causes that have brought us to the point where we are now. Slogans like "looking out for number one" just didn't appear haphazardly on the radar, they are real reflections of the heart of many. In an attempt to gain wealth and prosperity, many have taken a bribe from the enemy (Satan) and have sold their souls. Even though many leaders of our nation go to church and say some good things, they still have the same mindset that it's about them. Our nation has to get back to her foundational beliefs if we are to survive and prosper. Leaders have to turn back to God, the maker and creator of all things. They must repent and realize that they are nothing apart for Him. He has given us a blueprint for success called, the Holy Bible. We have to take Him at His word and know that by faith we can do all things through Him that loved us and gave Himself for us. No matter how far we have fallen and what it was that brought us to this point; we can be restored as a nation! Listen to the word of God; *"If My people who are called by My name will humble themselves, and pray and seek My face, and turn from their wicked ways, then I will hear from heaven, and will forgive their sin and heal their land." (2 Chronicles 7:14)*

PRAISE GOD! THERE IS A WAY TO TRUE RECOVERY!

INSERT RECOVER GRAPHIC

NATION + GOD = RECOVERY

There is much talk today about recovery, as I write this book we are just a few days removed from the tenth anniversary of 9/11, so a nation that is recovering is still fresh on millions of minds. Washington is constantly calling for economic recovery; various cities are calling for recovery from one kind of natural disaster or another. While these things are much needed, I appeal to you that we need a spiritual recovery, a recovery that will bring the hearts of man back to the Lord. What good does national debt reduction do to you as an individual if your soul is lost? I'm not saying that the nation's debt isn't a legitimate issue; I'm stating a fact that we should be more concerned with the recovery of our youth and men and women who have lost their way and their hope. This is what I know, not what I heard; there have been those who looked to have it all together, especially in the financial area. They had money, they had material wealth and they still chose to end their life by suicide. We desperately need to be recovered from ourselves. And we can began to do that by submitting our lives to the Lord and allow Him to do a restoration, or makeover if you will, in total being: body, mind, and spirit.

Remember that the one that I'm saying is willing and able to restore is the one that some want to remove from our currency. We want the blessings of God, but we don't want His name attached to what we are asking for. The nerve of those with this kind of mandate; you see, God doesn't have to do anything but remove His hand from us and we will be left to fall and suffer. I have tried to make it on my own, in my own strength, doing it my own way, only to fall deep and hard into a life of want and despair. The Lord sees what going on, He knows the condition of this nation and He hears the cries and prayers of His children. What has worked for me in my life, I believe, will work for a nation as well. We need to cry out to the Lord as a nation and repent! He will hear and answer our prayers. He is a Holy God who calls His people to Holiness. It starts with submitting to God and yielding to Him and by faith, trusting that He will do what He said. ***"God is not a man, that He should lie," (Numbers 23:19a).*** For this nation to bounce back, we must turn back to the God of Abraham, Isaac, and Jacob and we must come together in spite of party or denominational differences, because, a house that is divided among itself cannot stand. The sooner we understand that, the better.

The Bailout

During these tough economic times there has been much discussion on the topic of bailout. Many companies and institutions received bailout funds for the purpose of getting back on their feet. It was an attempt for businesses to maintain and work through a slow economy. However, we know that funds were misused by some lavish vacations and large bonuses were paid to top executives while they laid off other employees who lost not only the income, but also their homes and more. There should be a bailout for broken hearts, a bailout for souls to be restored, and a bailout those that have no hope and don't know what to do or where to turn. And I have good news for you, there is! Christ Said; *"Come to Me, all you who labor and are heavy laden, and I will give you rest. "Take My yoke upon you and learn from Me, for I am gentle and lowly in heart, and you will find rest for your souls. "For My yoke is easy and My burden is light."(Matthew 11:28-30)* This is the real bailout; Jesus has made a way because He is the way. After the funds that Washington has to offer dry up, what will people do? If they are too dependent upon it, they will compromise character, integrity, and their lives probably in ways that are destructive. Drug dealers, prostitutes, and murderers are not the only one s imprisoned. CEO's, Wall Street Executives, and Politicians have made their way there as well; because they want to "MAKE IT TO THE TOP." Listen to sound doctrine; *"But seek ye first the kingdom of God and His righteousness, and all these things shall be added to you."(Matthew 6:33)*

Priority is key, seek ye first the kingdom; we cannot be guided only by our intellect and worldly wisdom; but by the Spirit which will lead to righteousness.

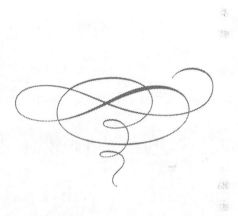

"Every way of man is right in his

own eyes, but the Lord weighs

the heart" (Proverbs 21:2)

CHAPTER THREE

Holiness and the Internet Age

Commercial internet service providers began to emerge in the late 1980's and 1990's. The internet was commercialized in 1995 and since that time has had a drastic impact on culture and commerce. With its emergence came near instant communication by electronic mail, instant messaging, voice-over IP, and the world wide web, with its forums, blogs, and various types of social networking. According to various studies, there was an estimated 1% of information carried by two-way communication; by the year 2000 the number had grown to 51%, and by 2007 more than 97% of all telecommunication was carried over the internet.

As is with anything, there is the ability to turn a good, positive thing into a negative one. Pornography, prostitution, child sex exploitation, drug sells, and all kinds of evil exist and are made easily available through the internet. Is this what the inventers had in mind at its conception? The internet carries with it a wealth of information that is now accessible at high speeds. With a click of the button of a mouse, you can have any type of information in front of you. There are positive aspects to the internet as well, such as the ability to study the Word of God and visit churches via their websites, get valuable information regarding medical, financial and occupational help. There is no doubt that this form of communication has moved us forward in many areas, but it has set us back in the area of morality.

Our children are being taught how to navigate computers and access the World Wide Web in elementary schools now, and are told early on that this is what they have to learn if they want to be competitive in the work place and in life. This ability, with the lack of parental supervision, (which we will discuss in another chapter) is a recipe for disaster. Adults and children alike are exposed to all types of sexual material through the internet and not all of it is sought after. You can do a search of something innocent and be bombarded with explicit material. This is one area that presents a serious challenge to men, women, boys, and girls alike; especially, when they maybe trying to live a godly life. The battlefield of Satan is the mind and whatever we allow our minds to take in has an impact on us. You cannot look at pornography and not have it impact your life. Our minds are like hard drives on a computer, images are stored and the enemy wants us to have that recall ability. He uses this at his time and for his purpose to tempt the individual especially when they are trying the move toward holiness. He wants to try and trap us into a life of sin, even if it is our secret and in our own mind. This is why we are encouraged by the Apostle Paul when he said; ***"Casting down arguments and every high thing that exalts itself against the knowledge of God, bringing every thought into captivity to the obedience to Christ." (2 Corinthians 10:5)***

Because of this exposure and even over exposure, lives are being ruined; males and females are dealing with sexual addictions in more and more numbers and at younger ages. I have seen this in my counseling practice and in my position as a police officer. The sad thing is that many don't see a problem with their involvement and preoccupation with sex. I have come to realize that this is a deep addiction and is often times more difficult to overcome than alcohol or drugs. We must get back to the basics of life, whereby we embrace innocence and purity. We must educate and encourage humanity to live a life that is pleasing to God, and to have intimacy with Him through a loving relationship with His Son Jesus Christ!

The internet gives us the ability to communicate around the globe from our offices, homes or wherever we are through broad banding and streaming, and with it comes another form of communicating that is so popular that is has become the norm. Texting is everywhere! If you can stop texting for a minute and observe this generation you will see fingers and thumbs moving "a mile a minute." It is so popular that someone can be in the same room with you and send you a text message instead of verbally communicating with you.

We have allowed this medium to dominate our homes and our lives; families seldom have sit down conversations with one another anymore. This has aided in children and parents being more and more disengaged. It has also played a part in illiteracy in this country. Kids and even some adults can send you text messages with all of the slang and lingo that goes along with it, but can't read or write at a normal proficiency for their grade level or age. We are a nation that is consumed with this vice, this along with video games is a large part of Americans time. This by itself is bad, now factor in that texting has being taking to a new level with what we know as "Sexting." Sexting is when a person or persons engage in explicit sexual conversation via their phones, usually in the text messaging mode, this is very popular between high school and middle school aged children, and to take it a step further, many take nude photos, or photos of themselves in some type of sex act so that it can be transmitted along with the text on their cell phones. Youtube is one of the most popular sites on the internet and all types of material are posted for anyone to see. There have been instances where people have come to file a police report because their images were posted on the web site. There is really nothing that law enforcement can do when the person was a willing participant and now because of being mad at the other party or some other reason, they now want the content removed. Please here me out, when your content is place on the web, in the internet world; IT IS OUT THERE FOREVER! I try my best to get people to understand this, especially young women. Some have been victimized and truly didn't know what was going to happen, but I'm sad to say that many did. Young women today want to be loved and admired and they will do just about anything to be accepted. Our young men are the same way, that's why you have a large participation in gangs in our society. What these kids are missing from home, they seek to find in the streets. They become involved, as some say, to feel wanted and loved. There are those that may not be involved with any kind of gang activity, but their wants and needs are the same, so they spent countless hours on social networking sites, such as; MySpace, Facebook, E Harmony, just to name a few. Many pass it off as it's just the way it is now and you're just old fashioned, but ask anyone, what is the most important part of a relationship and they will quickly and rightly say communication. Yet, very little time is devoted now days to communication that is not in some kind of electronic mode.

We must get back to face to face, get back to the dinner table or the front porch, whatever we have to do, to enhance our communication by content and not by speed because no electronic medium can fully capture ones heart or expression. You cannot, and do not get the same degree of assurance as when you are physically in the presence of someone and have eye contact with them. It may be a lost art form, but we need to find it in a hurry. Our children and our nation's future depend on it. What would happen if all of a sudden cell service went down, satellite communications fail, and the internet was shut down? How would we function?

Again, the internet and all of the things mentioned are not bad in themselves, societies use and perverseness is what's bad. Mankind has the uncanny ability to destroy everything that is made or invented. This comes from the destroyer of things, Satan. For the word says, ***"The thief does not come except to still, and to kill, and to destroy." But that's not the end of the verse; Jesus goes on to say, "I have come that they may have life, and that they may have it more abundantly." (John 10:10)***

Satan's influence is seen throughout the earth in television, music, clothing styles and yes even in the games that are played; more specifically video games. These games are being allowed to dominate a generation, especially the youth. They have become obsessed with playing video games and many at the expense of failing in school. The content of these games become more violent and explicit in nature each day, I believe that its one of the contributors to some of society's anger issues. I not saying that all games are sinful or of a corrupt nature, but we have to keep thing s in check if we want to live holy productive lives. You check them out for yourself, even some of the ones that appear to be o.k.

Why have we become so preoccupied with filth and degradation? Why do we choose to turn our heads and close our eyes to the fact that "things have gone south" and we have allowed it happen. We act as though we have no say in the matter of holy living, but the truth of the matter is we do. We cannot continue to touch such vile things and expect that we will be alright or to have an attitude that we can handle it. *"Can a man take fire to his bosom, And his clothes not be burned?" (Proverbs 6:27).* We cannot continue to play around with vices that are harmful and detrimental to our spiritual wellbeing. It is important to know and understand that there are hindrances in this life that absolutely destroy and or stunt grow and development in one's life. We can't afford to look at anything or listen to anything we want to because it causes us to become desensitized to the Spirit and voice of God. In this electronic age, with everything coming into our homes instantly by way of cable, satellite, or streaming through the internet, we are exposed to all types of materials and have access right at our fingertips. The challenge is to have the character of God working in us so that we can easily make the decision to turn the channel or turn the television or stereo off. I know that this dates me a little, but whatever it is; iPod, iPad, or wii, we must exercise control and authority over them and not be dominated or ruled by them.

These instruments have commanded a great deal of our time and attention; and it comes at the expense of valuable time that could be spent in a more productive way, such as with family, doing homework assignments or studying the Word of God. Time is valuable, and once it is gone we cannot get it back, so we must treasure it and make sure that we are being good stewards of it. Remember, we are responsible for the time that we are given, and we will be held accountable. Yes, accountability; I stated earlier that there is nothing wrong per se, with all of the new technology, it enables us to be very efficient in our occupations and in our homes, but we have to be on guard and not let the enemy trick or deceive us in its uses. There are times when no one else will be around and the enemy will tempt you to move into an area of ungodliness when you are surfing the internet; it is a great tool for research work, training. There are many Christian websites to help in spiritual development and guidance, but there are also too many evil and profane sites as well. For you who have a heart for holiness, I beg you to spend time in prayer before you even touch the computer. Pray that the Holy Spirit will lead and guide you as you access the World Wide Web; and not only should we pray for ourselves in this area, but also for our children and grandchildren, our family and friends because the majority of us use the computer now and have access to good as well as the bad.

Another problem related to this internet age is termed "Cyber bullying" and many kids and even some adults have found themselves victimized by this crime. Cyber bullying is a form of violence that can do lasting harm especially in lives of young people. This form of bullying is done by various forms of electronic communication; through email, social sites such as Facebook, blogs, text and instant messaging, and regular cell phone use. It particularly affects many adolescents and teens on a daily basis, and it is a serious part of the decadence in our society. Cyber bullies operate several ways: by spreading rumors online or through text, by posting hurtful or threatening messages on social networking sites or web pages or by sexting, or circulating sexually suggestive pictures or messages about a person. There many other forms that this crime can take and it can be very damaging; leading to anxiety, depression and even suicide. Statistics show that over half of the adolescents and teens have been bullied online and more than one in three have experienced cyberthreats. We must be mindful of this trend as we continue to use the internet and other electronic forms of communication. Identity theft is also very prevalent today and many are affected by it as well. Thieves and robbers are using the electronics too. This type of theft is one of the biggest problems that law enforcement faces today. Reports are being filed everyday from someone that has been victimized through identity theft. People are having their lives, jobs and families compromised by such evil schemes. We must be wise to take all necessary precautions when using the technology of today; there has to be an awareness that evil is ever present, but in spite of its presence, we must strive to live holy lives that bring glory to God.

If you or someone you know is experiencing any of these crimes be sure to inform your parents and or your local law enforcement agency. If people are silent on the issue, bullies and thieves will continue to perpetrate these crimes. As people of God, we must declare that we will not sit by and do nothing; but we will take a stand for righteousness and against the enemy that continues to threaten, and make a mockery of many in this world. So as you use all of the modern technologies that is available to you, do so with caution and do so with prayer. Satan has his plan for the use of this modern technology also, *"But as for you, you meant evil against me; but God meant it for good, in order to bring it about as it is this day, to save many people alive."(Genesis 50:20)*

For the most part, I have been speaking in terms of those that are victims, but maybe you are or have been one who perpetrated such crimes; if that is the case, I want you to know that there is still room at the cross for you. Call on the name of the Lord and repent of sin and the things that you have done, ask the Lord to forgive you, and if you are not saved, to save you. You must also accept His forgiveness and turn from the things that you were doing and turn to a life of holiness. It's not too late to turn things around in your life. Connect with God and commit your life to Him; you will be brought into a life of blessings and peace. And you will be enabled to use your technology skills for the Glory of God and the good for mankind. So go ahead, MAKE THAT CHANGE!

"Who ever goes to war at

his own expense?"

(1 Corinthians 9:7a)

CHAPTER FOUR

The High Cost of War

Make no mistake about it; we are a nation at war! And the other part of the truth is that war cost. You do not engage in warfare and not have a price associated with it. Since 2001, we have been at war in the Middle East; (Iraq, Afghanistan, and Pakistan). Our government has been committed to aid those nations that have been oppressed under terrorist leaders and dictators and those whom have threaten our land as well. We have supplied resources in this current war for ten years now, and have we made a change? The answer to that varies dependent upon who you ask, but everyone knows that the price has been tremendous. Right now it is projected that we will spend close to if not more than four Trillion dollars in this effort. What a cost? But that is just a financial or economic impact. There is another cost that has even a greater impact, the cost of our men and women who made the ultimate sacrifice by giving their lives for freedom, giving their lives for justice, and equality for others.

Over six thousand souls and counting have been mourned during this war. Families torn apart, dreams shattered, communities impacted and so much more that is associated with such lost. A high price indeed; but let me shift from the

Middle East to the wars that are been waged right here on our land, by our people, against our people. The drug war is still prevalent in this society, and the gang problem still exists. Even though there are those to try to down play their existences, gangs are and have been an increasing problem for cities and towns all across America. A 2009 threat assessment by The National Gang Intelligence Center states that most gangs formed in major cities expanded into neighboring communities during the 1970s, continued their expansion in the 1980s, and launched into full-scale migration during the 1990s. Initially many notable gangs such as Chicago-based Gangster Disciples, Black P. Stones, and Latin Kings formed for political and social reform during the 1960s. However, by the 1970s the focus of a number of the gangs shifted from reform to criminal activity for profit. This trend has stayed since that time.

In September 2008, gang membership was conservatively estimated at one million members, and based upon an analysis of federal, state and local law enforcement agencies, there are about 900,000 gang members residing within local communities across the country and more than 147,000 documented in federal, state, and local correctional facilities. According to the National Gang Center Office of Juvenile Justice and Delinquency and Prevention a 2009 survey which spanned 14 years estimates that that are more than 28,000 gangs. There is a war in this land. Not with tanks and aircraft, but with arms none the less. This type of war has also cost much, many of our teens and youth along with adults and even babies have fallen needlessly at the hand of gang warfare whether intentionally or unintentionally. We as a nation continue to suffer and see this nonsense and waste of life unfold daily. Moreover Hollywood has benefitted while glamorizing the gang and drug trade. I know because I was one that was impacted and caught up by the glamour back in the early 1980s when the movie "Scarface" came to the box office with Al Pachino's character "Tony Montana" there were many of us young men that wanted to be like him, we wanted to have what he had and live the life that he lived even though in the movie he died a violent death , we were captivated by what the drug world could provide and this only heightened our perception of what could be attained by a life of criminal behavior because we saw it in the real world as well. No part of our society is untouched by the affects of drugs and some criminal activity. One of the striking elements today is the age in which the kids are becoming involved. We have children killing children in this country, they are not fighting for freedom and equality, they are not fighting for a just cause, they are simply given over to a wayward society that seemingly turns its head and says "it's not my problem". Look at your local news and see if it's just a myth that I'm talking about.

In a study that compared 1998 to 2007, the percentage of homicides in which the contributing circumstances was gang-related increased from 22.0 percent to 32.7 percent, and now in 2011 the number is even greater. Gang and drug activity can be seen almost everywhere you go. These gangs like to stake out territory for themselves such as malls, theaters, and certain parts of the neighborhood. They attract and recruit young men and women to become a part of their organization by various means. They offer protection, money, jewelry, clothes, cars, and even guns. They give a sense of belonging to the individual and more than anything, deep down what is most drawing is acceptance. In talking with some of the youth today, that's what resonates with me the most, these kids want to be accepted and loved they not only want but need quality time and attention and when they don't get it at home from a loving family. They look elsewhere and put themselves in venerable positions to be used, manipulated, and abused physically, mentally, and emotionally. This is much more a cost than trillions of dollars; this is something that has a direct impact on our future. While this is not tanks, missiles, and camouflage, it is a war no less with far reaching ramifications in this country. We must realize that these gangs have become so sophisticated that some have blended in with "normal" society. They are not all wearing bandannas and baggie blue jeans, they are not all hanging on street corners; there are some who are doctors, lawyers and even some in our pulpits, so we cannot stereotype or we will surely misidentify many.

Our television does a lot of the mind preparation for them, through music videos and other shows that are watched by our youth in particular. There is a need to educate and reeducate if necessary to get the point across that the gang bang lifestyle, it's a lifestyle of destruction. *"Do not fret because of evildoers. Nor be envious of the workers of iniquity. For they shall soon be cut down like the grass and wither as the green herb. Do not fret because of him who prospers in his way. Because of the man who brings wicked schemes to pass." (Psalm 37:1-2, 7)*

There is nothing wrong with having material things; but there is something wrong with worshipping such things. There is a much better way that includes honesty, integrity, hard work, and the favor of God. One of the most transparent problems we face today is people, and especially young people, want everything right now without having to work for it or wait for it. They have a notion that they deserve to have what they want, when they want it; and many will do whatever it takes to gain material wealth, even if it means taking to a life of crime.

These people become blind to the reality that there are serious consequences and penalties that are associated with criminal behavior. Many have had to learn the hard way; others have paid dearly with their lives or the lives of their friends and/or love ones. No matter how much material wealth you amass, when you are gone to your grave, you can't take any of it with you. Jesus said, *"For what will it profit a man if he gains the whole world, and loses his own soul?" (Mark 8:36)*

As believers, we must live the life that Christ has called us to live. We must love and forgive; we must stand with courage and let the world know that even in this war we can win. Young men and women will ask what they have to do to gain some of the material things that they see others with, and we must have the answer, *"Trust in the Lord, and do good; Dwell in the land, and feed on His faithfulness. Delight yourself also in the Lord, and He shall give you the desires of your heart."(Psalm 37:3-4)*

This has to be conveyed to mankind everywhere; not black or white, rich or poor, democrat or republican, male or female, but all of humanity because it affects everyone. After we are through with our gang summits and drugs conferences, we need to get busy and demonstrate holiness by modeling a God centered life, regardless of what the President or Congress does or doesn't do. We are empowered to take back ground and save as many in this war as we can. You may ask how? I say, one life at a time, by being knowledgeable, courageous, and caring; and allowing God to demonstrate His love though us.

"Train up a child in the way he should go, and when he is old he will not depart from it" (Proverbs 22:6)

CHAPTER FIVE

A Great Dilemma: Parent or Friend

In this call to be holy in an unholy society, who has the responsibility to make sure that our children are receiving the nurturing and spiritual development that they need? Is it the schools? Is it the church? Is it from the coaches and mentors that they encounter during sports and extracurricular activities? While all of these are possibilities, I submit to you that they must receive it first and foremost from the home because none of the entities mentioned can replace or should I say, be required to replace the viable function of the home. And by home, I mean, the parents. Society is like it is in part because of the lack of good parenting at home. Communication is lacking, time and attention is lacking, as is the basic lessons of proper manners.

One aspect we see is, kids are having kids, and they are missing the basic fundamentals of parenting skills. Also when coupled with the fact that they are not really ready for the demands that rearing a child brings, true nurturing and development often take a back seat. There are some young mothers and fathers that think giving the child a bottle or something to eat and putting them in front of a television is all there is to know and therefore it is all they do; but parenting is so much more. The early years of a child's life are the most formidable years, and parents need to know how much or how little they are impacting a life. In my occupation as an officer, we get to see this more than we want to. We are called to homes everyday for a police matter only to find that it's more of a parenting matter. One of the problems is that there is a lack of discipline in the home, and this may be handed down from one generation to another. I hear it said so much by young people, "When I have kids, I'm not going to whip them or discipline them like I was discipline", and when that is the case we have a problem most time with their kids being unruly and disrespectful. We see these kids not only making bad choices, but also demonstrating bad behavior. They want to do what they want to do without any involvement from an authority figure, whether it is parent, teacher, or policeman. I have had several children in my office that had this mind set. Not all of them are a product of no parental involvement, some come from great homes and have good parents, but there are some who don't. There are those who have parents that have to work two jobs to make ends meet, some have to work odd hours and are not home with the child when there is a real need that they be there. There are those that choose to let cable and satellite raise their children, you may ask how I know? The answer is simple. I have witnessed it! Many Children are raised by MTV, BET, HBO, CINIMAX, and so on; or they are raised by video gaming systems. This shouldn't be!

One of the problems lies with parents wanting to be friends with their children to a fault. Many of the parents want be just like the kids; they don't want to grow up themselves, they want to act like, dress like, talk like the kids, they also want to listen to the same music, watch the same shows and there are some who want to share in the same friendships and relationships as their children. These individuals can't make the adjustment to true parenthood. Is there a place in our children's life for our friendship? Of course there is, but not to the point of where I see a lot of parents, these individuals are going through a crisis themselves, a lot of them are searching for their identity. This is probably in part to something that was never fulfilled in their childhood. There are those who try to live vicariously through their children, maybe it's because of something that they themselves did not get to do as a child and want so bad to do it that they live it out through the child. You can see this especially at the ball park on just about any Saturday morning or afternoon, or a weekday evening practice. The picture is that the child doesn't want to play sports but is forced to do so by the parents, the child is often put into these situations to feed the parents appetite for whatever sport or event it might be. So often what follows is anger and resentment from the child, not only toward parents, but others as well. We must learn to inspire, find out what interest and abilities our children have, and if it is not sinful, encourage and support them in that area. Our children need nurturing and mature guidance in their lives, rather than the father or mother trying to be "buddy buddy" with them. Remember this, if you are the buddy, then the child will have to look elsewhere for the true parental needs that he or she has.

As a society, we often look for others to be role models for our children; we look to entertainers, athletes, maybe even political figures for role models. I'm not saying that they shouldn't look for inspiration from someone if they aspire to be in that same field someday; what I am saying is that the parent should be their role models, not just occupationally, but a life model, a model that instills character, integrity, and values into the child's life. It's a great thing to see a child who idolizes their parents, who looks up to and respects them and honor them because they are keeping one of the commandment that God gave in the "Ten Commandments" *"Honor your father and mother, that your days may be long upon the land which the Lord your God is giving you."(Exodus 20:12)*. This just doesn't just haphazardly happen; it happens because time and proper parenting has been put into place, it also happens because in most cases there are proper lines established with in the family triad. There is balance and boundaries in place that make a healthy family and a happy one at that. This is not to say that there are not disagreements and challenges as there are with all families; but it is to be noted that clear lines of communication and trust are hallmark traits in these families, proper roles are carried out with the parent being the parent and the child being the child.

The word declares *"Behold children are a heritage from the Lord, the fruit of the womb is His reward."(Psalm 127:3)* they should be a blessing and not a burden to the parents.

So the dilemma is this; as a society, we have continued to move further and further away from godly principles and holy instructions. We have chosen, instead, to listen to what the world has to offer and thereby subjected our children and ourselves to chaos and calamity within the world we live. We have bought into the teachings of certain doctors and psychologists who have really given unwise counsel to many because they themselves have no relationship with the Lord and therefore cannot give the right instruction. They are limited to some classroom study at best, and fail do to the lack of spiritual wisdom and understanding; yet, many adhere to their words and advice and make them applicable in their lives. It is no wonder to why we are in the shape that we are as a society; because, we choose to ignore sound doctrine. God says that the wisdom of this world is foolishness; *(1 Corinthians 1:20)*. So no matter what kind of, or how many degrees one may have, or what university they have studied at, they are not fully equipped to address to the thing that is needed most in this society and that is holiness. Again, by holiness, I'm speaking of a lifestyle that will bring about change in one's life for the better, and thereby impact the lives of others and then more and more lives will be changed forever. We have set up ourselves for failure, our children and grandchildren are brought up thinking that it's all about them; they believe that they should get everything that they want right now! They fell that they are owed something just because they exist. Talk to the young folk these days and you will be able to see where I'm coming from, again the word entitlement come to mind. There are some great children in our world, those that choose to follow right teaching and wholesome instruction, but there are also many more which choose to live a disrespectful life with a bad attitude that challenges anyone in a position of authority.

We have to become grounded in the truth if we are to change this nation and our world, especially as it relates to our youth. The Apostle Paul in his letter to the church at Ephesus writes; *"Children, obey your parents in the Lord, for it is right. Honor your father and mother, which is the first commandment with promise; that it may be well with you and you may live long on the earth. And you, fathers, do not provoke your children to wrath, but bring them up in the training and admonition of*

the Lord." (Ephesians 6:1-4). How simple, yet profound; "bring them up in the training and admonition of the Lord!" not the television and radio talk show host, but the Lord!

I saw a sign once that read, do you know where your child is? And unfortunately many parents do not. I know because I have had to make the call to parents and ask them that question. Some believed that the child was in their bedroom, others stated that their child was spending the night with a friend and still others simply had no idea where the child was, and I gave the answer that he or she is in my police car. The expressions vary, some show anger, others shame, and the worst show nothing at all but have an attitude that I have somehow inconvenienced them. So what if my child is out after curfew, so what if they are participating in sex and underage drinking and smoking, this is their attitude. We have even had the parents admit that they bought or provided the cigarettes and alcohol for the child, and even knew that that child was involved in sex and a young age. They try to justify it by stating that the child is going to do it anyway, so they might as well provide a safe environment for them to do it. This is bad and becomes even worse by those parents that choose to participate along with the child. What kind of example is been set? They fail to realize that they are robbing these children of a childhood that can never be given back, and unless there is some type of intervention, these children will pass on this same type of learned behavior to another generation of their kids.

Where are the kids? Probably at the mall, if you have one in your area. You see these places have become low budget babysitters for parents, and with all of the ungodly things that are going on, it seems that people are either blind or just don't care about the kids. These children are dropped off and left for hours on end, left to just wonder around and do what whatever they want to do away from the parental supervision that is needed, and when an authority figure has to say something to one or any of them, they become the bad guys. When I deal with some of the parents that I have to deal with, I understand why the child acts the way he or she does. We must do better in our society, we have to do better.

There is a problem when the child is dropped off and the parents pull away, and the child heads to the bathroom and change into something more provocative and revealing I'm talking about young girls ranging in age from 9- 14. They tell the parent one thing and then do another. Parents, we must wake up and know what our children are doing; we can no longer sit back and just quote "well, you can't be around them 24/7." No we can't, that is why proper training and discipline are necessary, and godly instruction is crucial. There is an enemy that is trying to take them out, and I'm not willing to let him. These kids deserve a true chance at a real life, not some kind of fabricated TV reality show life, but the life that only the Lord Jesus can provide. There is godly instruction already in place, if we would just accept it and live by it, the scripture teaches us to *"Train up a child in the way he should go, and when he is old he will not depart from it." (Proverbs 22:6)* The problem is, many want to train them up in the way that they want them to go, and others want to train them up in the way that they went, but the bible says, in the way that they should go that is according to the word of God, according to the principles and precepts of God. He is our Father and creator and knows what is best for us.

Children must know and realize that God has purpose for their lives, that they were created for purpose and worship, it's not something that they have to wait own, the Lord will meet them right where they are. He is waiting for and willing to accept them now just as they are, as He says in Jeremiah, *"For I know the thoughts that I think of you, says the Lord, thoughts of peace and not evil, to give you a future and a hope." (Jeremiah 29:11)*. And the same goes for the adults as well; we must understand that we don't know all there is about parenting, and to be real, although there are many books available on the subject, most parents never read anything pertaining to parenting before they become parents.

We have been given the best resource in the word of God that will lead and guide us in this area, not only will it equip us to be good parents, it will also help us to be better people. If we trust and depend upon it, and have a proper relationship with the lord Jesus Christ, we will benefit greatly. We will establish the right relationships in life with our children and have the knowledge to pass on to them, the things that are needed and essential to live a life of holiness. In the process, we will be able to have the kind of friendship that is needed between a parent and child. Our families need prayer. We need fathers to be fathers and be the head of the home like they should be; fathers must know that they are the covering for the household. Not only are they supposed to be the natural providers of the home, but the spiritual providers as well. If fathers would become committed to the Lord and be the example for our families like we should, then things would turn around in our society. Young men would have someone to look up to and could begin to imitate their fathers who would state like Paul, *"Imitate me, just as I also imitate Christ." (1Corinthiains 11:1)*

There should be no dilemma; we can be friends with our children, but not at the expense of being parents. Parenthood comes first and a friendship should be birth from it. Our children need our love, they need our discipline, and they need our encouragement. They also need listening ears because the pressures and challenges they face today are real, and they need us to be there for them to help them through any situation that they may find themselves. Let's love them unconditionally like our heavenly Father loves us. Will they make mistakes? Sure we made some too, but someone cared enough to love us through them, and often times, that required that we be disciplined for our actions, but that's alright because that's what love does. *"My son, do not despise the chastening of the Lord, nor be discouraged when you are rebuked by Him; For whom the Lord love He chastens, and scourges every son whom He receives." (Hebrews 12:5b-6).* The scripture goes on to say, *"Now no chastening seems to be joyful for the present, but grievous; nevertheless, afterward it yields the peaceable fruit of righteousness to those who have been trained by it." (Hebrews 12:11).*

When we discipline our children we do it out of love, we do it with the hope that it will change behavior and that their lives will be impacted for the better. This is desperately needed today. I alluded to this in an earlier chapter, we have not only removed prayer from the schools, but have taken away the teachers ability and authority to properly discipline the children when they get out of line and misbehave. So we as a society reap the fruit of the decision by watching kids live out their life out of control without structure and respect for themselves or others. Something is wrong when children are allowed to talk back to parents or any other adults and disrespect them without any repercussions. Parents must take the lead in assuring that our children start out with a good foundation and basic fundamentals in behavior skills and manners, again ideally, they are with them the most in their formidable years. When parents allow a toddler to "throw a fit" and let them have their way, they should know that they are setting the stage for more bad behavior from the child as he or she gets older. I once witnessed a scene like this in a ToysRus store where a toddler wanted his mother to get him a toy plastic gun and she kept telling him no. The child began to get load and act out and then threw the gun and hit the mother in the face, it was as though she did not want to be embarrassed anymore, so she gave in to the child. In all probability, the child now believes that this type of behavior will get them what they desire. We must make sure that we don't reward bad behavior, and if bad behavior is shown by the child, then the proper discipline should be met out. What I observe these days is too much leniency and too little accountability. Yes, we must hold our children accountable for their actions, and this is something that they should be taught at an early age. So what is the role of the parents?

The father is the parent responsible for setting the pattern for the child's obedience in the family. Any discipline the mother does is an extension of the father's authority in the home. The husband and father must take the leadership in this area of the family, and the wife and mother must be in submission. In these days and time this is not what many want to hear, but it is right. The family is the oldest institution on earth and God set clear order and gave direct guidelines in His word concerning the family; but again, we have tried to change the order and meaning of a lot of things that God has said, and have tried to shape the word to fit our life style, instead of submitting ourselves to it. And therein lays the problem, mankind continues to think that he is wiser than God. Listen, the father is God's constituted home authority who is to discipline the child when he does or she does not obey as God intends. The father who does not discipline his children is a father who is undisciplined himself. You might say, but what about the homes where the father is not around? Then, by God's grace, mothers you will have to do what needed to make sure that the discipline is being met out. But just because the father isn't around, doesn't give the child a license to act up. A child's disobedience is not to be tolerated. It's not cute!

I know that this is a lot of talk on discipline, but trust me' we need it because it is right, and maybe we will be able to keep a child from being disciplined in the jail house. I have seen many with the attitude that nobody is going to tell me what to do, only to see their demeanor change when they enter into a correctional facility. Like it or not, they will do what they are told in there. We must bring our children up understanding accountability. This is one reason for this book, if we can keep one soul out of jail, if one soul can be brought to Christ; then, it is a success.

"You are the salt of the earth; but if the salt loses its flavor, how shall it be seasoned?

(Matthew 5:13a)

CHAPTER SIX

Give it Flavor!

Have you ever had something to eat that looked great, and smelled so good that you could almost taste it; but when you finally got settle and took the first bite, something was wrong. What looked so pleasing and smelled so wonderful had no taste, in other words, it was bland. Remember how disappointing it was and how it failed your expectations; you had an appetite, and had got your mouth ready only to have a letdown. When we speak of holiness in this society, sometimes it appears the same, things look good, but is really bland.

Believers must know and understand that we give the world flavor. It is the children of the Most High God that impacts the world so that it's not bland. With all of the different things there are in society, all of the different cultures, all of the entertainment, all of the social media and so on; you would think with this great mix that there would be enough flavor, but I say there is not because many are not being what we have been called to be, and that is the salt of the earth. Our Lord, in ministering to His disciples, gave what has been called the Similitudes; and in the first similitude He states **"You are the salt of the earth," (Matthew 5:13a).** We know that salt enhances the flavor of food, and it not only makes the dish taste better, it also aids in the preservation of the food because salt is a preservative. One definition states, "That which gives liveliness, piquancy, or pungency." We who are believers must realize that we should give the world flavor and in an unholy society, it should be evident when we are around or have been around. What I'm saying is that instead of the world making a big impact on the believer's life, the believer should be making a huge impact in the world. We have been given an awesome privilege to be able to season this society with the flavor of Christ. We have been equipped to make a difference in this world. Let's keep it real now, we in and of ourselves can add nothing that would change the flavor, because we ourselves, outside of Christ are of the same bland state. But with and through Christ we have the ability and the authority to change the flavor of the world. You may see this as being too big of a job for you and may ask how can I change the flavor of the world? Well, we need to break it down to one step at a time; we change it first by changing the flavor in our homes, and then our work places or schools, and then our communities and even in our churches. We bring flavor because of who we are in Christ. We have to understand that when we live godly lives, we impact our surroundings. We make a difference because of the Spirit of God living and operating in our lives, and we have to know that there are no limits to what the Lord can and will do through us is we allow Him to be God, and lead us by His divine will and purpose. You may or may not know that when you are a believer and are living a God centered life, and are in the workplace, He will bless the whole place because of who you are, why? Because you are the flavor there, you are what makes the place not only look good, but taste good as well. What am I talking about when I refer to taste? I'm speaking of the content and character of the place, the perception that one has when they encounter or do business in the establishment. And while all or not even the majority may live the God kind of life, God's favor can still be in the midst of it not because of them, but because of you.

The second part of that verse goes onto say; *"But if the salt loses its flavor, how shall it be seasoned?" (Matthew 5:13b).* This is one of the reasons that it's so important that we do as the scriptures say to walk worthy in the vocation to which you are called. When we speak of salt, we speak of something with the ability to change, and you cannot change anything when you are doing the same things; example: if you are using the same foul language that some of your co-workers are using its bland, if you are constantly late for work, that's bland. If you say you are a Christian and go to church but people in the workplace would never know it by your action, that's bland. I could go on and on, but you get the point. Anytime we say one thing and then do another to the contrary its bland and we have no seasoning to give. When I look at the world today, I have to say that it is in need of much salt.

Maybe you have had an encounter with someone who stated with their lips they were Christians, but you couldn't tell it by their actions; this unfortunately happens too often and is sad commentary. The world has to see that there is a difference, that there truly is a God and that he lives inside us. If our actions are the same as theirs, they will never comprehend that truth, at least not through you. There is a scene that has been played out in this world many times and especially in these latter years and it goes like this: a sports figure has been accused of using steroids or some other enhancement drug that is illegal to use, they deny any wrong doing, the vehemently tell the world through the media they are clean and have never used the substance that they are accused of using, "someone is just out to get them" they say. Next, there is a full blown investigation into the matter, with the athlete still persistently, clinging to their story. Testimonies and depositions are given, courtroom hearings are televised and then come the truth, and they now admit that they indeed did use the substance and apologize to everyone. There is need of salt in this situation. I know that in most of these cases, we are talking about the possibility of millions of dollars being at stake or a possible loss of a hall of fame induction, but it is still wrong and there are many of young athletes watching and maybe at a crossroads on whether or not to use such a substance. Know it or not, we make impact on the lives of others, whether positive or negative, an impact is being made. We are not on an island by ourselves, we operate in a society where we touch one another by the way we live, by what we say, and so on. When we speak of salt, we speak of an example to follow, a standard to live up to. We value and place a premium on things like, integrity, honesty, and loyalty. By loyalty I mean being loyal to the Lord Jesus. He is the one who died so that we might live. The scenario just mentioned is not exclusive to the sports world, we see the same thing on Wall Street with the CEO's of large corporations, with pastors and ministers in our churches, with teachers and administrators in our schools, with politicians and law enforcement officials, and every other arena. These things are happening all the time, so again I say that this world is in need of salt. A mother kills her newborn twin babies; another teacher is arrested for statutory rape of a student; a suspect kills grandparents and then set fire to the house, these are just some of the latest headlines from our area and are multiplied greatly when place on a national level. How long do we as individuals sit back and continue to live as if none of these things matter? As I stated earlier, we, as a nation, have seemingly become desensitized to all of the things that are going on, it's as though we thrown up our hands and given up to the mindset that "these things are just going to happen." What we need is more godly action and less lip service. Jesus said in quoting Isaiah; *"This people honors Me with their lips, but their heart is far from Me." (Mark 7:6)* It is not enough to talk about being a Christian, we must live it out. We are to be in the world, but not of the world. Go with the flow, that's a tune that heard all the time these days and far too much I might add. Being salt and bringing flavor to this world requires a discipline, a discipline that is attached to liberty and honor, I heard an older preacher say once "It's holiness or hell." I go out into the market place just as you do and see people enjoying themselves at the movies or at a restaurant and it looks like all is well, but who knows really other than the Lord. We have mastered the art of deception, to act like everything is good, when really, things are falling apart. We must learn to be honest with ourselves and others, there are a lot of people that feel that everybody is just like them, and then there are those that feel like nobody else would understand what they are going through. This could not be further from the truth; all of us have been through something, every experience we've had has not been good, and at the time, if we could have traded places with someone else we would have. We were taught in school, "we go through what we go through to help other get through what they are going through." This is another reason for the need of salt. Not all is bad, there are some good things going on in this world. I don't want to paint a picture of all gloom and doom. The good things also require salt; remember, salt is a preservative and we need much so that the good things stay good. There is a remnant, and the Lord always has somebody that is willing to be used for His kingdom and His glory. What is needful is a unified stance for righteousness, and the best way I think of to get flavor into this world is to start with our youth, instructing them in the way of holy living. Be prepared to answer when statements such as: "if I live holy it will be boring or I want be able to have any fun," these are false statements because I have more fun now that I have been saved. Does it cost something? Absolutely! it cost our Lord His life and He did it so that you and I could experience abundant living, so it's not dull or boring, but alive and fresh, with new mercies each and every day. The problem is that in most cases the idea of fun is flawed, you can have fun without drugs and alcohol and all of the other ungodly vices. The fun of the world has cost many lives and souls. Worldly fun has stunted and sabotaged individuals for years and years; it has robbed people joy and true peace and halted them from living their full potential. I was always told growing up that if you play with fire, you will get burned. I have been burned in my life, all in the name of having fun. Wasted time, wasted money, and wasted dreams all for worldly fun, but when the Lord touched my heart I began to find out what true fun was and continue to live in it now.

What a joy and privilege to be able to bring flavor into this world, what an awesome responsibility and treasure of Christ that He would tell us to go out and make a difference in this world. Remember, it's for Him, with Him and Through Him that we are able to accomplish this. Lives are at stake, so we must not procrastinate. We have to use our time wisely and make every day count. Giving flavor means having something to give, most of all it means giving love the Agape type of love which is unconditional. You can't hate people and bring any salt to the world, notice that I said hate people, there are some things that believers should hate, namely sin. Just as the Lord, we should hate sin, but love the sinner. There are some who seem to develop amnesia when they get saved. They act as though they have never done anything wrong and really have the wrong attitude concerning salvation. Theirs is "I got mine, get yours," they put down others and point fingers all the time, but when we are salt, we give flavor by understanding that we are called to the ministry of reconciliation, and we must be careful how we treat others considering ourselves as well. Although we are to go forward and not look back, we still have to remember where God has brought us from, and if He did it for us He can do it for others too.

I want to encourage and admonish you to begin to bring the salt to the table so that flavor can be added to this world, again we must start somewhere and I suggest we start small and work our way from there because you are not alone. If we all bring just a little salt, we will begin to make a difference and change the world.

The second part of the verse is: *"If the salt loses its flavor, how shall it be seasoned? It is then good for nothing but to be thrown out and trampled underfoot by men." (Matthew 5:13b).* Salt losing its flavor, how does that happen? One of the ways is by being out in the element too long. In this Christian life being out in the elements can equate to being away from the word and prayer, it can also be that you are away from fellowship with other believers. It can happen when you let down your shield of faith and become exposed to the open attacks of the enemy. Salt, when left out in the elements, especially in the region where Christ was at the time of this sermon, became hard and flavorless, but understand this, it had the same look, it was still crystallized and appeared to be good, but it had no taste. The only purpose that it served now was to put on the floor or walkway to prevent slipping. Taste gone, preservative qualities gone, the only use left was to be walked on by men. This is not what Christ has called us to, He has called us to great and wonderful things and the devil's place is to be under our feet. Again, just think how you feel when you expect something to taste a certain way, but it has no flavor, you become disappointed or even angry, and if it's something you bought you take it back and demand something else, or a refund of your money. This can also happen when we hang around the wrong people and are influenced by them instead influencing them. This is especially true for those who are new in the faith or babes in Christ. When you are first saved, there may be some people that you will have to cut off for a season, because of not being able to handle the temptations that were, in all probability, associated with them. To give you an example, when I was saved, I was delivered from alcohol I knew at that time that I was not strong enough spiritually to continue to hang around certain friends and even certain family, so I didn't. It wasn't that I thought I was too good or better than anyone, the Holy Spirit had given me enough wisdom to know that I couldn't handle it because I was still a babe, and hadn't learned how to bring my flesh under subjection. After a time of growth, I was able to go around them without any problem without being tempted by anything. I said this to show how one can lose flavor by hanging in the wrong environment. Let's say you are constantly around people who use profanity all the time, there is a good chance that you will also use the language at some time. We have to cherish our faith and walk worthy in it, knowing that our father gave us his best gift in the person of Jesus Christ, and it's in Him that we live, move, and have our very being. Most of us have a favorite seasoning that we like on our food. For a moment think of how your food tastes when that ingredient is added and how it enhances the dish and takes it to another level and gives it that "just right taste" umm. Ready, take a bite; now imagine it without the seasoning; that's what the Lord means when He says "you are the salt of the earth." The world has no taste without the believer. And to know that one day, we will be with Him for eternity in glory is simply wonderful. I believe being salt is an action phrase, it is a call to action to do and to be, again by a lifestyle that is pleasing to God. It is not just something that you do and become on Sunday, it is an everyday requirement of the Lord. When people are hypocrites, they loose the respects of others, and one thing that I have found out and it's this, people may not agree with you, they may not have a relationship with the lord, but if you are walking upright for the most part, they will respect you and what you stand for as long as you're not being one thing one day and something else the next. We are to be salt 365 24/7. Its seasoning, not seasonal; we can't take a break from it because it's vital. Lives are at stake and more things continue to happen on a daily basis.

Make a commitment to yourself and to God to give this world FLAVOR!

"You are the light of the world. A city that is set on a hill cannot be hidden."

(Matthew 5:14)

CHAPTER SEVEN

Light it up!

Darkness is defined as the absence of light or illumination; an unilluminated area; and the absence of moral or spiritual values. This is what is meant in terms of an unholy society. So much destruction and decay; everywhere you look there is darkness, not in the physical since, but in the spiritual since. I know this is somewhat cynical, but it is the absolute truth. A question was asked earlier of whose responsibility it was as it relates to our children, but who has the responsibility to check the moral compass of our society? Is it the White House? What about congress or the Supreme Court? With whom does the authority lie to enact change and impact lives? We have stated that there must be structure that begins at home, but I submit to you that the church has a vital role to play in the construction of a holy society. Listen to me; it is an absolute fact that darkness is changed when light is introduced to it. We say that this is a dark world in which we live, so where is the light? In this country, when you travel to different cities, you recognized that there is seemingly a church on every corner, and if not on every corner, then on every block. Nice structures, magnificent edifices, seem to be common wherever you go, but we still find ourselves as a society that is in a dark place. There will not be any light if we continue to erect buildings along. We can be a nation that mandates a church house be put on every other acre of land and still not have light. You see, the building does not produce the light that I'm talking about. No matter how many fancy chandlers you put into them, or how much stained glass it has. The structure doesn't have the power to command light into the lives of men. But yet, there seems to be so much emphasis place upon them in this age. I call it church wars because it seems that one church is trying to outdo the other when it comes to the church building. One church adds to their building, and the church across the street, not to be outdone, adds to theirs as well. One puts a gym on their campus, and the other puts an even bigger one on theirs. Is this what God wants? Is this what we are called to? Brick and mortar, wood and metal, glass and steel is all it is, and yes I know we dedicate these to the Lord, but often times they are just for our pleasure and bragging rights; say what you will, I know this to be the truth.

Jesus said that we are the light of the world, not the building, but the people who have a relationship with Him. This is where the impact is made, through the saints of God. Through those that have been blood brought and have a testimony to give to say that they too were once in darkness but have been brought to the light by the loving Lord Jesus. Light makes a difference in darkness; I have witnessed different degrees of light, and some are brighter than others but if you noticed even a little light can make a change in a dark place. Take for example, you are in a room with no light and someone turns on the light switch and the light comes on, the room is filled with light. Now say you are in the same dark room and this time you strike a match, you don't have the same kind of light, but you have some degree of light that you can find your way with. I will tell you now one of the main reasons for the lack of holiness in this unholy society, and it is this, ***The church has become too busy in trying to make light look like darkness!*** We have become occupied with trying to be like the world so that "we can win them", but the reality is, we will never win them by being like them. I know that the Apostle Paul says that I become all things to all men that I might win them. But don't take that out of context and we certainly have to consider the times. Darkness plus darkness equals more darkness, and hurting people who are going through something don't need to be presented with the same darkness, they need and want light. I believe with all my heart, the reason that the church tries to look like the world is they really haven't given up, or should I say, don't want to give up the ways of the world. For some it's something in it that they miss. The scripture tells us that men love darkness rather than light, so we already know that it is a serious challenge anyway. I'm trying to break this down as simply as I can; if you are hungry and I come to you and I am hungry too and have no money or food what can I really offer? The answer is nothing, that's what we have been trying to do in the midst of the church, but we have stuck the tag Jesus on it to make it appear holy. We don't need the appearance of holiness, we need the true essence of holiness being embraced and lived out in this world. What we see today is the people in church dressing just like the people in the world, women and even some men are seen wearing things to the church house that would be more appropriate for the night club. I heard someone say that it probably what they wore to the club the night before. Scantily clad women is bad enough anywhere, but to see it in the church is really a disgrace, saints we must have the courage to speak to these things. A young man wearing his pants below his butt is bad anywhere but in the church it is really ridiculous. Someone might say it's just the way things are now, and that's just the way the young folks dress, and what they're wearing these days. I say to them, we need a call back to holiness. We need to exercise our call to light, and again, light makes a difference, it doesn't try to stay the same, it makes a change in the situation and circumstances that it encounters. So we must to make an impact instead of trying to settle for and be like the world. I had some young folk tell me that the reason they don't go to church or feel that church is important is that it seems to be the same thing their doing now in their life.

The light of Jesus Christ brings glory to the father. Jesus doesn't need any gimmicks or worldly trends to draw people to Him, He said; *"and I, if I be lifted up, I'll draw all men unto me," (John 12:32).* We cannot lift Jesus up if we are in the same condition as the world. We shouldn't underestimate to power of the Lord Jesus. Somehow mankind feels that he has to somehow help Jesus out, so they come up with all kind of gimmicks and worldly tricks to make Him more appealing, "easier to swallow". The world has to know that Jesus died for its benefit not His, He was not, nor has He ever been lost. That distinction belongs to us; we were lost and in need of a savior, and He came down from Glory and died so that we could live. He came to redeem man to Himself by suffering on an old rugged cross, and in that process, He made a way for us to be light, not a dim light, but a bright light because we are a reflection of Him. People that are sick want to be healed; those that are blind want to receive sight, those that are hungry, want to be feed. This is why we can't offer them the same thing. Light is a part of a relationship with Christ and cannot be obtained any other way. You cannot go to school to get it; you can't go to enough church services to obtain it. It comes from a relationship! And when you have it, not only will you know, but others will know as well. *"A city that is set on a hill cannot be hidden." (Matthew 5:14b).* When we are brought into covenant with the Lord, He gives us a brand new life, a refreshing new beginning that has the empowerment of the Holy Spirit to make a difference in our life, and an impact on the lives of those we encounter. Light has the ability to reveal things because it allows us to see things that we couldn't see before. That's one of the amazing things about being born again, and walking in the light, I will use myself as an example: while I was in darkness, I thought I had it going on, I thought I was cool and had it together, but when light came, I found out just how ragged my life was and how un-cool I was because I was on my way to hell. Light allowed me to see the tattered and torn life I had, that I couldn't see in the dark. I know that I'm not alone, and that there are many others with this same experience. The blessing is that when the light comes sometimes its take a minute for our eyes to focus and see clearly for the first time what we really have around us. Now that I am saved and have matured in Christ, I can see things better, not only the good things, but the bad things as well. I have the ability see the great thing of the Lord, but I can also see the enemy clearer and better than I could before. That's what light will do, as the Apostle Paul stated; "we are not ignorant of his (Satan's) devices. What a blessing it would be if we could introduce light into the hearts at a young age and train our youth to command light in this society. The issues of peer pressure could be handled better, teen sex and teenage pregnancy would be dealt with differently, disrespect to parents and authority figures would be minimized, and society would began to turn around for the better. It could happen, but, it wont happen without believers beginning to live and call light into being by the authority that we have been given in Jesus' name and the power of the Holy Spirit operating effectively through us.

Substitutes this is what many are trying to walk in. they operate in something that has a semblance to light, but it is really not light at all. Today much attention is given to having a lot of programs and doing a lot of things and calling it ministry. Being busy doesn't bring light either; people, young and old, need to hear the truth as it relates to light. The darkness represents man in his sins and the only way that sin can be done away with is through repentance. We must call things as they are and not "sugarcoat" them; that is one of the things that plagues our society now, people seem to be very reluctant to tell others that they are wrong and need to make a change. What happens most of the time is, we see the action or the lack there of and want say anything to the individual(s); instead, we talk about it to others which really doesn't change anything. We have to speak to issues and ungodly behavior, we must challenge other brothers and sisters in the faith to come together, speak up and live as people of light. We all know that there is no one that's perfect on this earth, and we all have made mistakes in this life and failed God at times; so as it relates to light, we understand that the perfect light is in a perfect God. When we come into the new birth and become new creatures in Christ, we must understand, the old man has been crucified with Christ. The enemy loves to keep individuals trapped in their old life and many give into his nonsense simply through ignorance of God's word and the power there of. It makes no difference what the enemy brings up against you, how he recalls the things that you did in the past and the sins that you committed, if you are born again; you died and your life is hid with God in Christ Jesus! It is for and by that reason that you have the authority and the ability to command light in the midst of darkness. Glory to God! He saves from the gutter most to the utter most. Hallelujah to His name!

God spoke and brought order in the midst of chaos in the universe, and through His Son gives us the same opportunity in this world in which we live to bring the same order in the lives of mankind. Will we do as He commands? That is the big question that has to be answered.

Think for a moment about the future generations, now put it up against the back drop of our society today; much prayer is needed because if the course is not changed, all that await us is darkness. I use to hear people say that children are our future for tomorrow, and the more I live, the less I hear that been said. The reason is, we don't have the same confidence that we once had. We see so much disrespect from our youth and so much turmoil going on in the world right now that all many see is certain failure. But there is hope, and it can be found in the light. For that is what the light is; it is hope that things will change and that they can change. This is not about putting our youth of today down, I realize that there are some fine Christian young men and women out there that are very productive in this society, but I looking at the big overall picture where it seems like we're walking in dim lighting. I speak more so to the lack of leadership and mentorship for our youth. We cannot continue to think that somehow they will figure it all out on their own; you may say that that's what they think, but what they may think and what is reality are two different things. Trust me, I have children and grandchildren and understand how they can come off as knowing everything and really not having a clue about what's really going on. When I speak of darkness, I speak of the trappings that have a serious grip on multitudes but especially our youth. One of the instruments of darkness is video games, again, not all games are bad, but a lot of them are and the most popular ones that our youths love to play certainly are. On some of these games there is a rating that states "M" for mature, but you can go into homes around the country and find six, seven and eight year olds playing these games. I submit to you that it is more than just a game; it is a influence that seems to command more attention and devotion than parents are given. There is so much of an attachment to the games that most youth become sad and even depressed when they are not allowed to play them. All of the killing, stealing and adult situations that are a part of these games is mind blowing and what is more frustrating is that a lot of parents don't know or want even check the content to see what it entails. A common statement by some is they don't want to invade the child's privacy and therefore they don't go into the child's room to see for themselves what they are doing. You cannot play these things all day long and not be impacted by them. We cannot walk in the light and play with darkness. The scripture states;

"Rejoice, O young man, in your youth, and let your heart cheer you in the days of your youth; Walk in the ways of your heart, and in the sight of your eyes, but know that for all these things God will bring judgment. Therefore remove sorrow from your heart, and put away evil from your flesh, For childhood and youth are vanity." (Ecclesiastes 11:9-10)

I don't know of anyone who would give a child a gun and say, "go shoot yourself", but in essence, that is what we're doing when we don't monitor what the kids are into. We cannot shrug it off as just a game, this is where the leadership and mentorship that I mentioned comes in. There must be individuals who will take a stand for light's sake and will take time to make sure that people are led and pointed to the light. John declares in his first epistle: *"This is the message which we have heard from Him and declare to you, that God's light and in Him is no darkness at all. If we say that we have fellowship with Him, and walk in darkness, we lie and do not practice the truth. But if we walk in the light as He is in the light, we have fellowship with one another, and the blood of Jesus Christ His Son cleanses us from all sin." (1 John 1:5-7).*

I say again, it's all about a relationship with the Lord Jesus Christ, no matter how much some want to discount or discredit Him, only in Him, with Him, and through Him can we **light it up!**

"And that you put on the new man which was created according to God, in righteousness and true holiness" (Ephesians 4:24)

CHAPTER EIGHT

The New Man

Holiness, is it something that is really attainable? Can mankind really live holy lives in a world with so many demands and vices? Or is it just something to be achieved in a religious ritual? This writing is a call to holiness and yes it can be lived out right here in this present world, but it cannot be so without an understanding of the new man. You see, all of us have a past, we have something or some place that we have been delivered from, and those that have accepted the Lord Jesus into their heart have been born again. This means that you have been forgiven, cleansed, and made a new. One of the main things that Satan does is to mess with the minds of individuals to keep them thinking the same old way, so that they will continue to act the same old way.

For holiness to abound in this world there has to be a realization of the believer that the old man has been crucified with Christ. Yes the old man is dead! I know that many have been deceived into thinking that they will forever be the same creature as before but, God says, *"Therefore, if anyone is in Christ, he is a new creation; old things have passed away; behold all things have become new." (2 Corinthians 5:17).* It is imperative that we get this into our spirit because this is something that hinders the church in a great way. It speaks to the fact that many don't know who they are in Christ, and neither have they been able to tap into the resources and benefits of the new man. Walking in holiness and having an understanding that that old man is crucified is directly co-related. Assurance not arrogance is what I'm talking about. Yes to walk in holiness is challenging in this world and becomes more so as time goes by, but it's not impossible as some believe. As I said before, the battle ground is the mind, and our minds must be conditioned to what the word says about us and not what the world says about us. We must walk in the assurance that the old man is dead, and we are no longer controlled or dominated by him. It's easy to just sit back and listen to our flesh and give in to all kinds of temptations, but we must walk in the Spirit so that we fulfill the lust of the flesh. We understand that most of the things that hinder us in this society are flesh related or should I say geared toward the flesh? We are a society that thrives on the things of the flesh. We have come to live by the adage that "sex sells"; and therefore, it seems as though nothing can be advertised without it. Commercial industry says that it needs that kind of appeal, and so we can't even look at a hamburger ad anymore without it being linked to sex in some form or another.

I must admit, I love sports, but you cannot watch a sports program these days without your mind being induced with beer, alcohol, or sex commercials. I'm not saying it's wrong to watch a sports broadcast but you have to guard your heart and mind against the wiles of the devil because those images and influences have a way of taking you back to the old man, and if you're not careful you will find yourself doing the things that the old man use to do even if it is just in your mind. This is designed by the enemy, understand this; he doesn't want any holiness in this world and is crafty in planning and executing his plans and schemes to keep man in darkness. One of the most prolific ways he accomplishes this is by man not understanding who he is by the redemptive work of Christ. I can't stress it enough, the old man has to be crucified, and when you come to that realization you began to be empowered to do great things and overcome great obstacles in life. You began to operate in the newness of life and in the wisdom of God. You also understand that it is the work of Christ and not your work that brought this into being, and all you did was surrender to His will and walk in the authority that He provided. No matter how crafty Satan is, he is no match for the ALMIGHTY GOD! What has happened is he has tricked mankind time after time by deception and lies, and for the most part man bought a bill of goods that he should not have bought. But Jesus! Glory to God, made a way, and now through a made up mind, and the knowledge of God's word, we can walk in authority and in victorious living.

Holiness is a lifestyle; it is expressed in every aspect of our life, it is seen in our attitude, the way we treat others, in our giving, and the way we demonstrate our integrity and moral values. It is woven in our parenting or our obedience to parents, in the work place or when we are at play, holiness is who we are, not just something we do. It is based upon the fact that we are new creatures in Christ Jesus, and that our sin debt has been paid in full. The more we come to grasp this knowledge the better we will become in our society. This teaching must be passed along, it should be preached, taught, and modeled so that we can indeed affect a change in the lives of others. It makes no difference what your occupation is; whether you are Caucasian, African American, Asian, or Hispanic or any other nationality, whether you are rich or poor. Every one of us has the opportunity to live holy lives that pleasing to God, but we must make it our choice to do so. God has made us free moral agents to choose between right and wrong, and between good and evil. I have heard people all of my life saying that it was so hard to live a Christian life, but the word of God says that the way of the transgressor is hard. When you are a believer of the Lord Jesus Christ, you walk in liberty and freedom and can do all things through Him that will give you strength. To live in the new man is to live by the Spirit of God and not by the flesh. *"Therefore, brethren, we are debtors- not to the flesh, to live according to the flesh. For if you live according to the flesh you will die; but if by the Spirit you put to death the deeds of the body, you will live. For as many as are led by the Spirit of God, these are sons of God." (Romans 8:12-14)*

Holiness requires a choice to be made between the Spirit and the flesh, and it may seem easier to live in the flesh, but to live in the Spirit is so much better and so much more rewarding. Imagine what this world would be like if the masses began to walk in holiness, crime would be down; citizens would not have to fear as they do now, and children would have an even better chance at growing into productive citizens and leaders of our communities and our nation. Partying, drinking, drugging, and smoking seem to be the only way that many think they can have fun or a good time; and trust me; I was there too at a point in my life until I found out that there was truly something better. Now I know that not only can you have a good time, but you can have the best time of your life in the security of a loving savior. When you're drinking, for example, you forget what happened and often get so drunk that others have to tell you what happened. Think about it; that's not a good time, that's a foolish time. Because you don't know what could have happened to you or to someone else, especially if you were driving.

Life is about more than that; it is about love and fulfillment that only come through Jesus Christ. It's about trusting, about helping, life is about giving and when I say that, I mean giving of yourself and making sure that you are living a life of significance and are leaving a good legacy when you are gone from this earth. Life is about training others to operate in freedom and not bondage, it's about caring enough to pass on to and not pass by those that are hurting and in need. Life is about holy living! In the community that I live in we have a motto that says; Live, Work, and Play; this is to sell the fact that we are a growing community that has a vision of people being able to not live, but also work and enjoy the rest and relaxation through various means of play and entertainment. Think about how much better that sounds when you add the aspect of holiness to it. It excites me to know that as good as we think we have it now, it can be so much better in the light of holiness. We must learn to walk in the new man, understanding that we, no matter how long we have been in the church, were once dead just as many others are today, and the Lord saved us and gave us new life, listen; *"But God, who is rich in mercy, because of His great love with which He loved us, even when we were dead in trespasses, made us alive together with Christ (by grace you have been saved), and raised us up together and made us sit together in the heavenly places in Christ Jesus, that in the ages to come He might show the exceeding riches of His grace in His kindness toward us in Christ Jesus.(Ephesians 2:4-7).*

Glory to God! He made a way for us. Trust me, not only are we able to experience the joy and benefit of this when life on this earth is over, but we can walk in this truth right now.

As we are challenged to live holy lives in an unholy society, we must concentrate on the new man because the old man cannot produce the right things for effective holy living. You know like I do that things look better when they are new, they feel better when they are new, they smell better when they are new, and so it goes with us, the new man is better and has the ability to positively impact the society in which he is a part of. Again, there is so much filth and degradation in this world right now, but I also believe that there is a remnant that is committed to living holy lives and walking in the light and truth of God's word.

We have a choice, we have a say as to the type of society that we will live in, we don't have settle for anything. If it's not right, we need to speak up and stand up for what is right, remember that choice may have a lasting impact, and may set precedence in a given situation. There is no shortage of church houses that I can see, no matter where I go and what city I go to, I see an abundance of church buildings, but we don't see an abundance of holy living. Allow the new man to come forth and make a difference in this world. There is so much talk about loss in this time and age, everyday in the news there is talk of loss of jobs, homes, businesses, and marriages, suicides are more and more frequent and it seems as though hope is being loss everywhere and people are giving up, we who are saved must become encouragers and have the courage to reach down, and reach out to those who are down and hurting.

This is simply a call to be real and live out your life in a holy way, it is a call to wake up and stand your ground in a society that says you don't have any ground. It is a challenge to believers and a invitation to unbelievers. It is a word of hope, a word of change to say that things can be better and lives can be impacted for the better even in this society. It's a call for men to be better men and fathers to their children and husbands to their wives, for women to be virtuous and better mothers. It's a call for children to be obedient, and to honor their parents, and live a life of respect, a call to stand in the midst of adversity, and declare the power of the Almighty; and He has empowered us to do it!

Remember, the old man has been crucified and the new man has been raised in the newness of life. A powerful scripture that believers must get in their spirit is found in Paul's letter to the church in Colosse that says, ***"For you died, and your life is hidden with Christ in God" (Colossians 3:3).*** To live holy, impactful lives in this society requires that we indentify and live by the ways of the NEW MAN.

"Let us hear the conclusion of

the whole matter: Fear God and

keep His Commandments"

(Ecclesiastes 12:13)

The Conclusion

This is what I believe, I believe that Jesus Christ is the Son of God. I believe that He was born of a virgin, that he lived a life in a physical body and as the word declares, was tempted in all points just as we are, yet without sin. I believe that He hung, bled, and died that we might have a right to eternal life, and rose early on the appointed morning in victory and all power. I believe that He ascended back to heaven and is seated at the right hand of God the Father making intersession for us. This is what I believe, and because I believe it, I also believe that the born of God can live holy lives in an unholy society. I believe that mankind yearns for something that is higher than himself, but many just don't realize that what they yearn for is The Lord Jesus Christ, who offers to all, life everlasting.

Faced with the many challenges of this life, I believe we can live lives that bring glory and honor to The Most High God. Jesus lived in difficult times as well, and faced with many things, He choose to honor His Father by being obedient even to the death on the cross. We must renew our hearts and minds to live out our faith in the midst of adversity and trying times. Where would we be today if the saints of the early church had given in or given up. They suffered many things, even death, for the gospel sake. When rulers and emperors said no, they said yes! Many were beheaded, burned, tortured beyond measure and crucified, yet they held fast to their faith. We are not experiencing that level of persecution in this country at the moment, we have a freedom and a liberty that they only dreamed of, and so we should be excited about the opportunity to live out our faith. Though we might be talked about, laugh at, and persecuted, we must not forget that we are more than conquerors. There is a great reward for living a life of holiness, and not just when we have left this earth and gone to glory, but in this present world we will be blessed and our lives made richer through the acts of obedience.

The conclusion of the whole matter is to fear the Lord and Keep His commandments; this becomes possible when you have made Jesus the Lord of your life and surrendered your life and will to Him. Know this; you can honor the Lord in every aspect of your life by aligning your life with His word. When this happens, you will realize that everything you do can be an act of worship to Him and because certain laws and principals are in effect, such as the law of sowing and reaping, those seeds that you sow will bring a harvest and an impact will be made on this society.

The word perilous is defined as: dangerous, threatening, exposed, vulnerable, risky, unsure, hazardous, unsafe, precarious, and chancy. All of these fit into the framework of the definition of our society; but thank God, He has made a way to overcome these and become victorious just as He is. Will it get better? I know that it can't get better without His sovereign care and the acceptance from individuals of Him. For in Him lies all the answers, the joy, peace, and the satisfaction of life, all of these rest securely in Him and with Him. So, if you don't already have a relationship with Him, now is a great to start. He is the author and finisher of our faith, and He is waiting and willing to meet you right at the very point of your need. Trust Him and commit to Him to live godly in these perilous times.

Something to think about The Paradox of Our Time in History (Anonymous)

The paradox of our in history is that we have taller buildings but shorter tempers, wider freeways, but narrower viewpoints. We spend more, but have less, we buy more, but enjoy less. We have bigger houses and smaller families, more conveniences, but less time. We have more degrees but less sense, more knowledge, but less judgment, more experts, yet more problems, more medicine, but less wellness.

We drink too much, smoke too much, spend too recklessly, laugh too little, drive too fast, get too angry, stay up too late, get up too tired, read too little, watch TB too much, and pray too seldom. We have multiplied our possessions, but reduced our values. We talk too much, love too seldom, and hate too often.

We've learned how to make a living, but not a life. We've added years to life not life to year. We've been all the way to the moon and back, but have trouble crossing the street to meet a new neighbor. We conquered outer space but not inner space. We've done larger things, but not better things.

We've cleaned up the air, but polluted the soul. We've conquered the atom, but not our prejudice. We write more, but learn less. We plan more, but accomplish less. We've learned to rush, but not to wait. We build more computers to hold more information, to produce copies than ever, but we communicate less and less.

These are the times of fast foods and slow digestion, big men and small character, steep profits and shallow relationships. These are the days of two incomes but more divorce, fancier houses, but broken homes. These are days of quick trips, disposable diapers, throwaway morality, one night stands, overweight bodies, and pills that do everything from cheer, to quiet, to kill. It is a time when there is much in the showroom window and nothing in the stockroom. A time when technology can bring this letter to you, and a time when you can choose either to share this insight, or to just hit delete. Remember; spend some time with your loved ones, because they are not going to be around forever. Remember, say a kind word to someone who looks up to you in awe, because that little person soon will grow up and leave your side. Remember to give a warm hug to the one next to you because that is the only treasure you can give with your heart and it doesn't cost a cent. Remember, to say, "I love you" to your partner and your loved ones, but most of all mean it. A kiss and an embrace will mend hurt when it comes from deep inside of you. Remember to hold hands and cherish the moment for someday that person will not be there again. Give time to love, give time to speak and give time to share the precious thoughts in your mind.

This was something that was shared with me found on the internet, again just think about the truths that it speaks to. Maybe you are like me, I'm not perfect, and I know this is not a perfect world, but the God I serve is perfect and has a perfect plan for my life and yours as well. So let's slow down and take time to enjoy one another and the creation that He has made, remember we can experience some of heaven right here on earth. As with any relationship, communication is key; Prayer is essential to holy living and we all need it while we are on this journey. May God bless you and may His abundance be yours!

Godly Wisdom for Godly LivingWords from Proverbs

Chapter 1:1-9
Chapter 2:1-33
Chapter 3:1-20, 31-35
Chapter 4:1-27
Chapter 6:16-19
Chapter 8:12-21
Chapter 10:1-12, 27-32
Chapter 11:14, 27-31
Chapter 12:1-8
Chapter 14:1-3, 12, 25, 34-35
Chapter 15:1-6
Chapter 18:19-24
Chapter 22:1-17
Chapter 31:10-31

The proverbs of Solomon the son of David,
King of Israel:

To know wisdom and instruction,
To perceive the words of understanding,
To receive the instruction of wisdom,
Justice, judgment and equity;
To give prudence to the simple,
To the young man knowledge and discretion—
A wise man will hear and increase learning,
And a man of understanding will attain wise counsel,
To understand a proverb and an enigma,
The words of the wise and their riddles.
The fear of the Lord is the beginning of knowledge,
But fools despise wisdom and instruction.
My son, hear the instruction of your father,
And do not forsake the law of your mother;
For they will be a graceful ornament on your head,
And chains about your neck.
My son, if you receive my words,
And treasure my commands within you,

So that you incline your ear to wisdom,

And apply your heart to understanding;

Yes, if you cry out for discernment,

And lift up your voice for understanding,

If you seek her as silver,

And search for her as for hidden treasures;

Then you will understand the fear of the Lord,

And find the knowledge of God.

For the Lord gives wisdom;

From His mouth come knowledge and understanding;

He stores up sound wisdom for the upright;

He is a shield to those who walk uprightly;

He guards the paths of justice,

And preserves the way of His saints.

Then you will understand righteousness and justice,

Equity and every good path.

When wisdom enters your heart,

And knowledge is pleasant to your soul,

Discretion will preserve you;

Understanding will keep you,

To deliver you from the way of evil,

From the man who speaks perverse things,

From those who leave the paths of uprightness

To walk in the ways of darkness;

Who rejoice in doing evil,

And delight in the perversity of the wicked;

Whose ways are crooked,

And who are devious in their paths;

To deliver you from the immoral woman,

From the seductress who flatters with her words,

Who forsakes the companion of her youth,

And forgets the covenant of her God.

For her house leads down to death,

And her paths to the dead;

None who go to her return,

Nor do they regain the paths of life—

So you may walk in the way of goodness,

And keep to the paths of righteousness.

For the upright will dwell in the land,

And the blameless will remain in it;

But the wicked will be cut off from the earth,

And the unfaithful will be uprooted from it.

My son, do not forget my law,

But let your heart keep my commands;

For length of days and long life

And peace they will add to you.

Let not mercy and truth forsake you;

Bind them around your neck,

Write them on the tablet of your heart,

And so find favor and high esteem

In the sight of God and man.

Trust in the Lord with all your heart,

And lean not on your own understanding;

In all your ways acknowledge Him,

And He shall direct your paths.

Do not be wise in your own eyes;

Fear the Lord and depart from evil.

It will be health to your flesh,

And strength to your bones.

Honor the Lord with your possessions,

And with the firstfruits of all your increase;

So your barns will be filled with plenty,

And your vats will overflow with new wine.

My son, do not despise the chastening of the Lord,

Nor detest His correction;

For whom the Lord loves He corrects,

Just as a father the son in whom he delights.

Happy is the man who finds wisdom,

And the man who gains understanding;

For her proceeds are better than the profits of silver,

And her gain than fine gold.

She is more precious than rubies,

And all the things you may desire cannot compare with her.

Length of days is in her right hand,

In her left hand riches and honor.

Her ways are ways of pleasantness,

And all her paths are peace.

She is a tree of life to those who take hold of her,

And happy are all who retain her.

The Lord by wisdom founded the earth;

By understanding He established the heavens;

By His knowledge the depths were broken up,

And clouds drop down the dew.

Do not envy the oppressor,

And choose none of his ways;

For the perverse person is an abomination to the Lord,

But His secret counsel is with the upright.

The curse of the Lord is on the house of the wicked,

But He blesses the home of the just.

Surely He scorns the scornful,

But gives grace to the humble.

The wise shall inherit glory.

But shame shall be the legacy of fools.

Hear, my children, the instruction of a father,

And give attention to know understanding;

For I give you good doctrine:

Do not forsake my law.

When I was my father's son,

Tender and the only one in the sight of my mother,

He also taught me, and said to me:

"Let your heart retain my words;

Keep my commands, and live.

Get wisdom! Get understanding!

Do not forget, nor turn away from the words of my mouth.

Do not forsake her, and she will preserve you;

Love her, and she will keep you.

Wisdom is the principal thing;

Therefore get wisdom.

And in all your getting, get understanding.

Exalt her, and she will promote you;

She will bring you honor, when you embrace her.

She will place on your head an ornament of grace;

A crown of glory she will deliver to you."

Hear, my son, and receive my sayings,

And the years of your life will be many.

I have taught you in the way of wisdom;

I have led you in right paths.

When you walk, your steps will not be hindered,

And when you run, you will not stumble.

Take firm hold of instruction, do not let go;

Keep her, for she is your life.

Do not enter the path of the wicked,

And do not walk in the way of evil.

Avoid it, do not travel on it;

Turn away from it and pass on.

For they do not sleep unless they have done evil;

And their sleep is taken away unless they make someone fall.

For they eat the bread of wickedness,

And drink the wine of violence.

But the path of the just is like the shining sun,

That shines ever brighter unto the perfect day.

The way of the wicked is like darkness;

They do not know what makes them stumble.

My son, give attention to my words;

Incline your ear to my sayings.

Do not let them depart from your eyes;

Keep them in the midst of your heart;

For they are life to those who find them,

And health to all their flesh.

Keep your heart with all diligence,

For out of it spring the issues of life.

Put away from you a deceitful mouth,

And put perverse lips far from you.

Let your eyes look straight ahead,

And your eyelids look right before you.

Ponder the path of your feet,

And let all your ways be established.

Do not turn to the right or the left;

Remove your foot from evil.

These six things the Lord hates,

Yes, seven are an abomination to Him:

A proud look,

A lying tongue,

Hands that shed innocent blood,

A heart that devises wicked plans,

Feet that are swift in running to evil,

A false witness who speaks lies,

And one who sows discord among brethren.

I, wisdom, dwell with prudence,

And find out knowledge and discretion.

The fear of the Lord is to hate evil;

Pride and arrogance and the evil way

And the perverse mouth I hate.

Counsel is mine, and sound wisdom;

I am understanding, I have strength.

By me kings reign,

And rulers decree justice.

By me princes rule, and nobles,

All the judges of the earth.

I love those who love me,

And those who seek me diligently will find me.

Riches and honor are with me,

Enduring riches and righteousness.

My fruit is better than gold, yes, than fine gold,

And my revenue than choice silver.

I traverse the way of righteousness,

In the midst of the paths of justice,

That I may cause those who love me to inherit wealth,

That I may fill their treasuries.

The Proverbs of Solomon:

A wise son makes a glad father,

But a foolish son is the grief of his mother.

Treasures of wickedness profit nothing,

But righteousness delivers from death.

The Lord will not allow the righteous soul to famish,

But He casts away the desire of the wicked.

He who has a slack hand becomes poor,

But the hand of the diligent makes rich.

He who gathers in summer is a wise son;

He who sleeps in harvest is a son who causes shame.

Blessings are on the head of the righteous,

But violence covers the mouth of the wicked.

The memory of the righteous is blessed,

But the name of the wicked will rot.

The wise in heart will receive commands,

But a prating fool will fall.

He who walks with integrity walks securely,

But he who perverts his ways will become known.

He who winks with the eye causes trouble,

But a prating fool will fall.

The mouth of the righteous is a well of life,

But violence covers the mouth of the wicked.

Hatred stirs up strife,

But love covers all sins.

The fear of the Lord prolongs days,

But the years of the wicked will be shortened.

The hope of the righteous will be gladness,

But the expectation of the wicked will perish.

The way of the Lord is strength for the upright,

But destruction will come to the workers of iniquity.

The righteous will never be removed,

But the wicked will not inhabit the earth.

The mouth of the righteous brings forth wisdom,

But the perverse tongue will be cut out.

The lips of the righteous know what is acceptable,

But the mouth of the wicked what is perverse.

Where there is no counsel, the people fall;

But in the multitude of counselors there is safety.

He who earnestly seeks good finds favor,

But trouble will come to him who seeks evil.

Whoever loves instruction loves knowledge,

But he who hates correction is stupid.

A good man obtains favor from the Lord,

But a man of wicked intentions He will condemn.

A man is not established by wickedness,

But the root of the righteous cannot be moved.

An excellent wife is the crown of her husband,

But she who causes shame is like rottenness in his bones.

The thoughts of the righteous are right,

But the counsels of the wicked are deceitful.

The words of the wicked are, "Lie in wait for blood,"

But the mouth of the upright will deliver them.

The wicked are overthrown and are no more,

But the house of the righteous will stand.

A man will be commended according to his wisdom,

But he who is of a perverse heart will be despised.

The wise woman builds her house,

But the foolish pulls it down with her hands.

He who walks in his uprightness fears the Lord,

But he who is perverse in his ways despises Him.

In the mouth of a fool is a rod of pride,

But the lips of the wise will preserve them.

There is a way that seems right to a man,

But its end is the way of death.

A true witness delivers souls,

But a deceitful witness speaks lies.

In the fear of the Lord there is strong confidence,

And His children will have a place of refuge.

The fear of the Lord is a fountain of life,

To turn one away from the snares of death.

Righteousness exalts a nation,

But sin is a reproach to any people.

The king's favor is toward a wise servant,

But his wrath is against him who causes shame.

A soft answer turns away wrath,

But a harsh word stirs up anger.

The tongue of the wise uses knowledge rightly,

But the mouth of fools pours forth foolishness.

The eyes of the Lord are in every place,

Keeping watch on the evil and the good.

A wholesome tongue is a tree of life,

But perverseness in it breaks the spirit.

A fool despises his father's instruction,

But he who receives correction is prudent.

In the house of the righteous there is much treasure,

But in the revenue of the wicked is trouble.

A brother offended is harder to win than a strong city,

And contentions are like the bars of a castle.

A man's stomach shall be satisfied from the fruit of his
mouth,

From the produce of his lips he shall be filled.

Death and life are in the power of the tongue,

And those who love it will eat its fruit.

He who finds a wife finds a good thing.

And obtains favor from the Lord.

The poor man uses entreaties,

But the rich answers roughly.

A man who has friends must himself be friendly,

But there is a friend who sticks closer than a brother.

A good name is to be chosen rather than great riches,

Loving favor rather than silver and gold.

The rich and the poor have this in common,

The Lord is the maker of them all.

A prudent man foresees evil and hides himself,

But the simple pass on and are punished.

By humility and the fear of the Lord

Are riches and honor and life.

Thorns and snares are in the way of the perverse;

He who guards his soul will be far from them.

Train up a child in the way he should go,

And when he is old he will not depart from it.

The rich rules over the poor,

And the borrower is servant to the lender.

He who sows iniquity will reap sorrow,

And the rod of his anger will fail.

He who has a generous eye will be blessed,

For he gives of his bread to the poor.

Cast out the scoffer, and contention will leave;

Yes, strife and reproach will cease.

He who loves purity of heart

And has grace on his lips,

The king will be his friend.

The eyes of the Lord preserve knowledge,

But He overthrows the words of the faithless.

The lazy man says, "There is a lion outside!

I shall be slain in the streets!"

The mouth of an immoral woman is a deep pit;

He who is abhorred by the Lord will fall there.

Foolishness is bound up in the heart of a child;

The rod of correction will drive it far from him.

He who oppresses the poor to increase his riches,

And he who gives to the rich, will surely come to poverty.

Incline your ear and hear the words of the wise,

And apply your heart to my knowledge;

Who can find a virtuous wife?

For her worth is far above rubies.

The heart of her husband safely trusts her;

So he will have no lack of gain.

She does him good and not evil

All the days of her life.

She seeks wool and flax,

And willingly works with her hands.

She is like the merchant ships,

She brings her food from afar.

She also rises while it is yet night,

And provides food for her household,

And a portion for her maidservants.

She considers a field and buys it;

From her profits she plants a vineyard.

She girds herself with strength,

And strengthens her arms.

She perceives that her merchandise is good,

And her lamp does not go out by night.

She stretches out her hands to the distaff,

And her hand holds the spindle.

She extends her hand to the poor,

Yes, she reaches out her hands to the needy.

She is not afraid of snow for her household,

For all her household is clothed with scarlet.

She makes tapestry for herself;

Her clothing is fine linen and purple.

Her husband is known in the gates,

When he sits among the elders of the land.

She makes linen garments and sells them,

And supplies sashes for the merchants.

Strength and honor are her clothing;

She shall rejoice in time to come.

She opens her mouth with wisdom,

And on her tongue is the law of kindness.

She watches over the ways of her household,

And does not eat the bread of idleness.

Her children rise up and call her blessed;

Her husband also, and he praises her:

"Many daughters have done well,

But you excel them all."

Charm is deceitful and beauty is passing,

But a woman who fears the Lord, she shall be praised.

Give her of the fruit of her hands,

And let her own works praise her in the gates.

Special Thanks

To David and Jeannie Davis (ohlas), for all of the love and support throughout the years, we will always be family, Love ya! To Sgt. Tyler Chandler for all of your help, support, and the sincere dedication and professionalism in which you operate. To Mrs. Debbie King for your cheerful spirit, willingness to help and your support. To my Pastor, Dr. Bobby and Sis. Barbara Sanders and the entire Corona First Baptist Church Family, thanks for all of the prayers, love and support that you have giving me down through the years. I am forever grateful and love you deeply. To Pastor Larry and Ann Grainger and the Abundant Life Church Family, it is a blessing to work, and worship together with you. May you continue to fight the good fight of faith; I have much love for you guys. To Pastor Tim and Angie Bryant and the Grace Fellowship Family, God brought us together and it is an honor to serve with you. We have much work to do, but as the song says "Ain't no stopping us now"! To Pastor Walter Phillips Jr. and the United Kingdom of Believers Family for loving me and never giving up. "From Hopewell to Heaven"! Love you man. To Dr's Ron and Diane Hamm and the Cedaridge Church Family, for all of the insight, instruction in learning, and the friendships, keep on keeping on in the work of the Lord. To Rev. Greg and Nancy Roberson, thank you for the prayers, support, and love that you continue to give, stay on the watch wall. Also a special thanks to Dr. Willie Bryson, my comrade and friend, we've come a long way, and we still have a long way to go. It has been a blessing to be on this road with you, through ups and downs you've been there; you have shown yourself as a faithful friend and brother, I am forever indebted to you. Much love to you and Pam and your family. To Elaine and (Howard) Jackson, for the seeds that you've sown into my life and ministry. Also to David and Malani Stephens and family, for all your support and help.

There are so many that have deposited into my life, that I can't name them all right now; you know who you are, so I say to those that are mentioned and those who are not; I love you with a love unconditional, may God's favor and peace be with you and may you receive a double portion and more back for all that you have given to me. Look up and be watchful, for our redemption draws nigh!

A Special Thanks To Maristone at Providence Curt Revelette, CEO.

About the Author

Dr. James A. Hambrick is a native of Nashville, TN.; He and wife Denise currently reside In Mt. Juliet, Tn. where he currently serves as Pastor of counseling and development at Grace Fellowship Ministries. He has spent twenty-five years in the gospel ministry. He holds a B.A. in Christian Education, a Master's and Doctorate in Psychology & Christian Counseling. He is also a 2009 graduate of Northwestern University's Police Staff and Command School. James is employed with the City of Mt. Juliet as the Assistant Police Chief and also serves as Chaplain. He is board certified in the areas of; Integrated Marriage and Family therapy; Death and grief Therapy; and Crisis and Abuse Therapy. James is well respected in the community and abroad, and is sought out for counseling, seminars, and preaching engagements. He is a member of several organizations including; the National Christians Counselors Association, Tennessee Association of Chiefs of Police, and International Association of Chiefs of Police. He and Denise have five children and eleven grandchildren.

References

http://www.nationalgangcenter.gov/content/Document/
History-of-Street-Gangspdf James C. Howell, John P. Moore,
National Gang Center Bulletin, May 2010.

National Gang Center Office of Juvenile Justice and
Delinquency Prevention and Bureau of Justice Assistance.
http://en.wikipedia.org/wiki/Internet#History

Visit James at:
www.jamesahambrick.com
Follow Him on:
Facebook or Twitter